TOWPATH GUIDE

D1329337

Living Aboard

Nick Corble and Allan Ford

First published in 2008 by
The History Press
The Mill, Brimscombe Port,
Stroud, Gloucestershire, GL5 2QG
www.thehistorypress.co.uk

Reprinted in 2009

British Library Cataloguing in Publication Data.
A catalogue record for this book is available from the British Library.

ISBN 978 0 7524 4519 9

Typesetting and origination by
The History Press
Printed and bound in England.

Contents

The Authors

There is not much Allan Ford doesn't know about narrowboats. Not only does he live on one himself, but he has also spent many years servicing and fixing them. His experience ranges from the mechanical through to the minutiae of day-to-day living, and he brings this to life in these pages, offering hints and tips and helping the potential liveaboard to avoid some of the more obvious, and some of the less obvious, pitfalls of life afloat, as well as ideas on how to get the most out of this uniquely attractive way of life. This is Allan's second book, his first being *Riding the Wall of Death*. Also written with Nick Corble, this book chronicles the history of the motorbike fairground attraction, his other great passion 'the Wall of Death'. His email is indianscoutrider@hotmail.com.

Living Aboard is Nick Corble's fourteenth book and his eighth for Tempus, including the popular *Britain's Canals: A Handbook*, which should be seen as a companion to this volume. Series Editor of the Tempus Towpath series, Nick specialises in the canals but has also written a biography of the great engineer James Brindley, as well as more broadly on the English countryside. Nick is also a regular contributor to the national and local press on a range of topics and examples of his work can be found at his website www.nickcorble.co.uk. His email is nick@nickcorble.co.uk.

Introduction

There is something terribly romantic about living on board a boat. The sense of independence, of being able to drift away at a time of your own choosing, of quite literally being one's own master have probably all appealed to most of us at some point. Being an island surrounded by water must also make a difference. Already separated from the rest of the world, what could be more natural than going one step further and casting yourself off from the rest of conventional society?

Every year many thousands do just that, with many tens of thousands more contemplating the same. It is a little-known fact, for example, that more people live on a boat in London than do so in Venice, and the same is true for places such as Oxford and Birmingham too. Making sure that the dream doesn't become a nightmare is what this book is all about.

Buying a boat and living on it is a relatively simple task, but understanding and coping with the practicalities of living aboard is something that tends to come with experience. This book condenses decades of experience of living aboard and sets it out into easy-to-follow chapters. Not everything can be taught, and often there is no substitute for learning the hard way, but this book offers a number of short cuts and checklists to help you get the most out of your time spent living aboard.

Living in a conventional home has its own subconscious rules and routines – knowing where the stopcock or the fuse box is, when to put the bins out, who owns which fence – and it is much the same when living on board a boat. The secret is getting to know these rules and letting them become second nature.

It has been estimated that over 15,000 people live aboard a boat in the UK and, like their boats, these people are all different. Some choose to live afloat by preference, others for convenience and still more because they have little choice but to do so. Some stay there permanently, and others for part of the year only. Some never stray from their moorings, while for others constant movement is the very point of being on a boat. Whilst these considerations may colour different individuals' priorities, there are some challenges that face them all, and this book is all about meeting those challenges.

Living Aboard is published as part of the growing Tempus Towpath series, with its sister volume *Britain's Canals: A Handbook* a particularly useful companion, offering an insight into areas as diverse as navigation tips, paintwork and how to get the most out of the canals. The emphasis in these pages is on more hard-nosed practical advice for those looking to make their home on the water.

The focus here is on those looking to live aboard on our inland waterways. But this is not meant to exclude those who choose to live on board along our coasts. Much of the advice given here is equally relevant to them, although inevitably living with tides, saltwater and our sometimes harsh coastal climate brings its own additional challenges. In line with the Tempus Towpath format we do not claim that the advice given in this book is totally comprehensive, but we hope that we answer most questions, whilst the Learn More and Links section at the back provides some signposts on where to go for further information.

The information we provide in this book is based largely on years of experience, although we acknowledge that it is entirely possible that certain regulations or recommended best practice may alter in the time between us writing this book and you reading it. Our thoughts are necessarily subjective, and we would always recommend that anyone contemplating a life afloat talks to as many knowledgeable people as possible – we are happy to admit that others may hold different views to ours, but hope that in these pages we give enough sound advice to set you on your way.

Living aboard offers a host of pleasures, but isn't for everyone. If it turns out to be for you, we hope that this book makes some small contribution to making your life better once you finally get afloat. If you have any suggestions for any future editions of this book please feel free to contact either of us at the email addresses given above.

Finally, we would like to thank the following for their time and assistance in compiling this book, and in particular allowing us to photograph them at work: Tooley's Boatyard, Banbury; Oxfordshire Narrowboats, Heyford Marina; Kingsground Narrowboats; Safeshore Marine; British Waterways; Jez Boat Painting Services; Mike Walker Boat Services, Ayhno Wharf and Midland Chandlers, Braunston. All the photos in the book are by the authors unless otherwise indicated.

Chapter 1
The Floating Citizen

Living aboard a boat is something many people contemplate at some point in their lives, although only relatively few ever actually make the leap. There are a number of reasons for this, both practical and psychological. The purpose of this book is to lay these reasons out, to allow those thinking about a floating home to make an informed choice.

Given the book's practical focus, it may seem that the list of potential obstacles and bases to cover begins to snowball to a point where you may conclude that only the most foolhardy would ever contemplate a life aboard. That is not the intention. Rather, the aim is to guide you through the issues a potential liveaboard needs to consider, so that living aboard becomes a dream, not a nightmare.

Having said that, if the negatives accumulate to a point where the balance of consideration leans rather too heavily into the debit column, then it's likely that you lack the temperament, skills, finances or simply the appetite to make a success of life afloat – and these pages will have saved you a lot of anguish, and possibly just as much cash!

If, on the other hand, you remain undaunted by the challenges covered here, and maybe even feel energised by them – and we hope you are – then the book will also have done its job, helping to equip you for a successful future afloat, and hopefully allowing you to bypass some of the more obvious mistakes.

In considering a life afloat, it is the practical challenges which are in many ways easier to meet, since very few of the problems that you might encounter will not have cropped up before, and if you are reading this, it is probably precisely because you are keen to learn from the experience of those who have 'been there, done that'. The psychological side of things is harder to pin down, and whilst the rest of this book focuses on the practical, this opening chapter is more about the fundamental considerations of joining the liveaboard community.

Do you prefer solitude?

If you are lucky enough to have the choice of whether to live aboard or not (and we recognise that for some this may be a case of Hobson's choice), then a few minutes' contemplation of these wider issues is ultimately going to be much cheaper than splashing out tens of thousands on a boat, and then finding out that you were unsuited to it all along.

The good news is that wanting to live afloat is not the first sign of madness. To put things in perspective, a population at least equivalent to that of Reigate – that's nearly twice the size of the average UK town – lives on boats in the UK. Unlike the inhabitants of Reigate, however, it is easy for this population to become forgotten citizens. Unlike the town-dweller, they cannot take for granted those facets of modern life that we have come to assume as the basics of a civilised society, such as on-demand electricity, gas, water, sewage and telephone. Whether moored or moving, the boat-dweller – metaphorically and sometimes literally – takes the conscious decision to cut themselves off from these amenities, and perhaps less consciously, from much else that society offers.

What previously simply arrived or was taken for granted is now something that has to be actively pursued. Some of these 'rights' are more tangible, such as basic services and utilities. Securing these is relatively straightforward and your options for doing so are covered in subsequent chapters. Others are more difficult to pin down, and may only become apparent on an ad hoc basis, or in times of crisis, but are just as important as components of a civilised lifestyle, and these are discussed later in this chapter.

The most important place to start, however, is a consideration of what sort of person you are and the type of environment you are likely to be comfortable in. Whether you are the social type or a bit of a loner (and the liveaboard community tends to weigh disproportionately towards the extremes of the spectrum) is likely to have a huge bearing on your lifestyle afloat. If you have the choice, and if it's possible to find out beforehand, understanding the type of people who like particular kinds of moorings may be critical in choosing where you want to be. Marinas, for example, tend to have more of a community feel, whilst a mooring out on its own is, by definition, more isolated. This assumes, of course, that you want to have a base, even if you do not spend all of your time there. As later chapters will show, this may not necessarily be the case.

If a more isolated setting is your preference, then it is worth contemplating the different degrees of isolation. Being a well-watered island means that there is no shortage of options when choosing where you might live afloat, be it a marina, canal, river or coastal estuary, but ours is also a compact island and most of these are close to some kind of civilisation and you'd have to be fairly determined to cut yourself off completely. The first question to ask, therefore, is whether you are the sort of person who needs daily contact with others, or whether you're quite happy with your own company.

Taking the issue of sociability to the next level is the question of whether you want to live alone or share your boat with others. Again, this is not always a matter of choice, but it is a matter worth consideration. Boats are, by definition, confined spaces and depending on who's on board, this will have different implications. If you are on your own – and this tends to be the majority amongst liveaboards – is this something you are comfortable with, or is there even a slight potential for 'cabin fever'? If you are with someone else, how much do you all need 'your own space' every now and then? It's something that needs to be planned for if you live on a boat.

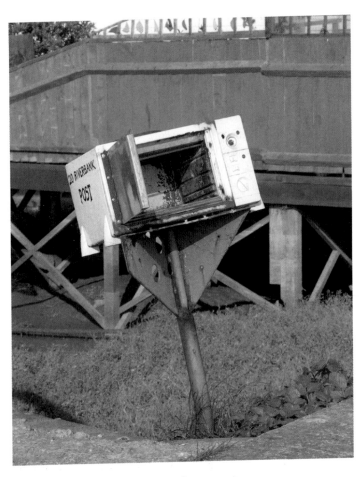

You may need to make arrangements for your post.

Motivations for living aboard are probably as varied as the number of people who do so. That said, there are some further considerations probably worth pondering. Is life afloat something you regard as a permanent or a temporary state? If it's the latter, you may wish to at least think about how you are eventually going to return to dry land. For example, some live aboard to coincide with a particular time in their lives – a short-term job, for example, or perhaps while they are studying. Others may do so through a lack of alternatives, driven by an event such as a divorce or a shortage of funds, and then find themselves trapped with no way of returning to a 'normal' way of life in a house. But as we will see, 'normal' has a way of redefining itself when you choose a boat as your home.

Deeper, less spoken-about factors may also influence your decision. Ask yourself why you want to live aboard – is it a romantic dream? Is it part of a long-cherished retirement plan, the true motivations for which are rooted in mythology, and you now find yourself in a position where it's impossible to back out? Is it a way of avoiding a bigger truth? None of these is probably enough on their own to see you through even the medium term, and if circumstances allow, it can be a good idea to sit down and try to articulate exactly why you want to choose this way of life, and maybe ask a close friend to listen to it and challenge you. Whatever your conclusions, you should be under no illusions. Making the choice to become a liveaboard represents a dramatic shift in lifestyle, which in anyone's language is not something to be taken lightly.

That said, living aboard offers real benefits that compensate for the inevitable compromises that you will have to make. The trick is not to see these as second-best, just different. Making the psychological adjustment to being a permanent liveaboard is something that takes at least a year, and probably a minimum of two winters. It involves acquiring a new set of habits and expectations from life, and gradually, a fresh perspective dawns, creeping up on you so that others begin to notice the changes in you more than you do yourself. You value things differently, both the tangible and the intangible; you appreciate aspects of your environment you either took for granted or hardly noticed before; and, like someone deprived of their sight, gain a heightened sensitivity to other aspects of your personality. It's not an instant conversion though, and too many potential liveaboards give up before their epiphany. So when things aren't going so well, remember that this is a long-term commitment and something that has to be worked at.

Assuming you're still game, the remainder of this chapter considers those issues that lie somewhere between the purely psychological and clearly practical. These include matters which are generally considered rights in a civilised society, but which may have to be worked at to be secured. What is more, the ways of achieving them may vary from area to area, leading to a lack of certainty that may, according to your predisposition, be either extremely frustrating or all part of the fun!

Let's start with the most basic consideration of all: your health. A life lived independently and largely outdoors, with a fair sprinkling of physical labour, seems at least reasonable for one's health, and the popular image of life aboard is one that is good for you. What happens when things go wrong though, especially if you are on your own? What if you are far from the nearest road and an ambulance, doctor or nurse can't get to you?

Liveaboard boats can even have an 'upstairs'!

It's worth bearing in mind that life aboard is inherently more dangerous than life in a house, at least until you've got the hang of it, and the potential for catastrophic events is very real. The misery of even niggling complaints can multiply when you've only your cabin and a bunk to see them off in, and when keeping warm means getting out of your bed to stoke the fire, or worse, having to go outside to fetch some coal or change a gas bottle. The potential hazards of 'cabin fever' have also already been mentioned, and the danger of mental illness should not be dismissed, especially for those whose motivations for living aboard were complicated in the first place.

On the practical side, there's also the consideration of where you stand with regard to accessing health services, something we would never question if we lived on dry land. The NHS is not necessarily geared up for those of 'no fixed abode' and if you are not careful there is a danger that you can involuntarily elect to become a 'non-person' by choosing a life afloat. Of course, hospitals will admit you if something disastrous occurs, but what if your needs are more ongoing – the management of a chronic complaint, for example – or if you need the less intensive services of a GP? GPs are not obliged to accept you onto their rolls, and may decide that the prospect of boat visits should you fall ill is not something they relish. Even if they were willing, registration may not be practical if you intend to be on the move for significant lengths of time. Yes, there are drop-in health centres and clinics, but you need to know where they are, and advance notice may be necessary if any prescriptions are likely to be needed.

Similar thought also needs to be given to access to other parts of the welfare state such as pensions, post offices and social services, and special consideration is needed if you intend to live aboard with small children or with pets. If you think it may be difficult getting access to a GP, this is nothing compared to gaining access to a dentist or a vet, especially if it is an emergency.

All this is not to underestimate the value of support mechanisms within the boating community. Depending on your circumstances, but following the 'there but for the grace of God' principle, fellow-boaters tend to be more than willing to help out a neighbour in distress. If you are known on a mooring it's unlikely that you will have to worry about someone looking after your boat if you are called away, but if you aren't, this may be a consideration.

Continuing the floating citizen theme is the issue of making your voice heard. Every citizen has a right to vote unless they are a peer or are in prison. But if you are a liveaboard – the ultimate 'floating voter' – it may seem at times as if a third category has been added. To vote you must be registered in a particular area, which may be tricky if the area you are living in changes most days. Postal voting is one option, but has to be organised.

Equally, being a citizen carries responsibilities and one of these is to pay taxes. The authorities may be slow to grant you your vote, but you can be pretty certain that they'll be a lot quicker in claiming your contribution. One particular area of potential complication is council tax. The rules of this tax are open to a host of different interpretations by local authorities, and if you are thinking about a permanent mooring, it is worth checking out the local situation. Luckily, the Residential Boat Owners' Association provides a cheap and useful paper on this very subject (see 'Learn More and Links').

Another intangible is communications. Being on the move or down a gated towpath may make it difficult for the postman to reach you. In practice, boaters tend to be a resourceful bunch when it comes to collecting their post, but this isn't something that happens automatically. Options may include a 'care of' host address, for example at a marina, or a PO Box, but bear in mind that the daily rattle of the letter box may become a thing of the past if you live aboard.

Of course some might argue that this doesn't matter as post is becoming a thing of the past (despite statistics to the contrary), and may welcome a way of avoiding the increasing menace of junk mail. 'Email is the future' may be the rallying cry, but here too you should not assume that access is easy. Broadband in particular can be a problem, especially if you have to access it from a mobile phone, and Wi-Fi access remains lamentably poor in this country compared to our European neighbours – but this is an issue covered in more depth later in this book.

A side-effect of not having a regular address is the difficulty that this can cause with banking. Banks seem to be obsessed with customers having a fixed abode and the utility bills to prove it. As a result, assuming you don't go for the 'holding address' option, it can be a good idea to create your own version of 'offshore' banking before you make the leap away from bricks and mortar. Bear in mind the issues already highlighted with Internet access, since although online accounts may offer a good option in the future, they are probably not there yet. Notwithstanding connection issues, passing your financial details over a wireless system isn't necessarily a good idea.

Post offices have also represented a possibility in the past, but with the closure of so many smaller branches in the pipeline their main virtue – their coverage – is in the process of being taken away. ATMs are likely to offer the best way to get cash out of your account, but again these can be subject to charges, so take care. One idea may be to have a number of accounts with different institutions and set up standing orders into them from a central account on a regular basis.

On the subject of phones it might be thought that mobile technology has solved this problem, until you consider the fact that most boats are made of steel and steel and mobile signals do not go together well, even taking into account the variability of signal we still seem to suffer from. Anyone for that important call from the bank standing outside in the rain balanced on the gunwale? This is before you consider matters of cost.

Room To Rent in Luxury Houseboat

- Lovely room to rent in furnished flat on a houseboat at Shoreham.
- Unusual home with most mods (central heating, washing machine; TV with digibox etc, **broadband** negotiable) & no Cons!!!
- Share large kitchen/living room & bathroom (inc shower) with 1 woman & friendly dog
- Fully Furnished
- Lots of storage space in good sized bedroom
- Quiet, relaxed home for longer term rental
- **Available end of March for £360pcm & bills and deposit**

One option is to rent.

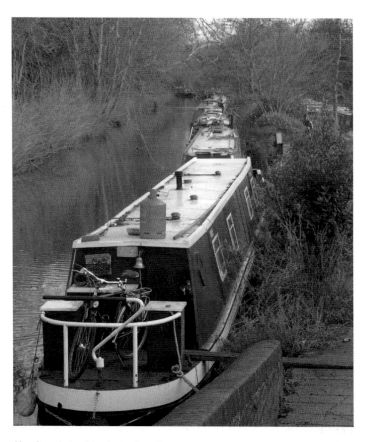

Liveaboards tend to cluster together.

You may have to be prepared to 'rough it' a bit!

These perspectives assume of course that boaters are seeking to replicate life on dry land on their boat. It is just as possible that those who choose a life afloat are also selecting a life away from instant access and constant nagging: freedom from calls suggesting that your life is incomplete without double glazing, a life away from prying eyes and CCTV (although most marinas have CCTV these days).

As with most things, the secret lies in achieving a happy balance but, at the risk of being repetitive, and as subsequent chapters will demonstrate, this is something that has to be worked at. Living aboard involves a new set of rules, rules that you need to flex into, not fight. You need to start out from the viewpoint that compromises will have to be made, the question is which are the things you are prepared to sacrifice the most easily and which are you prepared to go the extra mile to achieve?

Someone once made the analogy between someone who becomes a liveaboard but constantly complains that things aren't what they're used to with someone who decides to become a vegetarian but keeps buying mock-meat products. The secret to being comfortable with the liveaboard lifestyle lies with the three 'A's: accept its rules, adopt its mentality and adapt it to suit your own particular needs and desires. If this is something you think you can do the rest of this book will, we hope, prove to be invaluable.

QUESTIONS FOR THE FLOATING CITIZEN:

- What is your motivation for wanting to be a liveaboard – is it a necessity or a choice? How much room for manoeuvre do you have? Have you or your partner ever had a holiday afloat?

- Do you enjoy practical challenges?

- Are you used to 'roughing it' occasionally – have you enjoyed camping or caravan holidays in the past?

- How much do you need daily contact with other people?

- How much do you and possible companions value your 'personal space'?

- Are you likely to need good access to health and social support?

- How comfortable are you about a partial 'opting out' from mainstream society?

- How much do you need 'instant' access to the wider world?

Chapter 2
Choosing a Boat

Having made the decision that you want to live on the water, the next step is to think about what type of boat you want. Of course, as anyone operating on a budget knows, 'want' is not necessarily the same as 'need' and putative liveaboards will soon discover that finding the right boat involves a lot of compromise and not a little foresight.

Buying boats is not like buying houses. Any estate agent will tell you that the three most important factors involved with buying a house are location, location and location; but when it comes to liveaboard boats, this is only true if you are planning a permanent mooring. When buying a boat there are many different factors involved, but the issue of whether you intend to stay put or whether you intend to cruise – and if you do, how much cruising you intend to do – will probably be one of the most important factors in deciding which type of boat you get.

This question is critical on a number of levels. If you do intend to cruise, then you will need to consider your motive power and the compromises this may force. Most boats require an engine, unless they can be entirely powered by sail or muscle power or are not required to move, and this means an engine room or compartment and somewhere to store fuel. This affects the configuration of your boat and will become especially important if your boat is also your home, due to considerations of noise, space, vibration and fumes.

Just as importantly, your decision on whether or not to cruise will affect the three fundamental questions that the potential liveaboard will need to settle. These are explored in greater detail below and are:

- What type of waterway do you want to be on?

- What type and size of boat will suit you best?

- Are you looking for a boat, a house or a houseboat?

Tidal estuaries tend to offer a home to more permanent craft.

TYPES OF WATERWAY

As has already been highlighted, there is no shortage of places where you can live on a boat on our small island. Four main types of waterway offer a berth: canals, rivers, coasts and estuaries. Each of these offer their own advantages and disadvantages. Being 'dead water' without tides, canals are highly predictable, and although disasters such as breaches or floods do occur they are highly unusual. They are also well geared up for the liveaboard, with plenty of marinas, moorings and other facilities, and on the canals you are rarely far from the other conveniences of modern living such as banks, supermarkets and launderettes.

Canals' detractors would point out that these features make them all too predictable and even complain of overcrowding in places. The decision of whether or not to cruise also comes in here, as those who do want to wander will find in canals a ready-made network; even if, once again, the canals' detractors might be scornful of the pre-packaged nature of the waterways system, with its designated routes and hordes of amateurs and tourists clogging things up for half the year.

Canals also, by their very nature, determine the type of boat you can have. In order to cruise the entire network you will need to have a narrowboat, no more than 6ft 10in wide, although if you are happy to limit yourself to the broad canals you can double this. Most narrowboats are 30ft, 44ft, 50ft, 60ft or 70ft long, although the northernmost English canal, the Leeds & Liverpool, has locks that only allow boats of a maximum 60ft in length.

Rivers offer greater scope for boats, but less freedom to cruise. They may also be tidal, which adds another challenge to the choice of moorings and to the range of kit which needs to be carried, such as anchors and lines. Taking the Thames aside, rivers tend to be less busy, but locks can be more of an issue, as can moorings, and they tend to be busier generally. If you have a craft that can cope with coastal waters, however, they can offer a good compromise.

Coastal waters themselves tend to be a whole different ballgame. These are obviously tidal and berths for the liveaboard can be hard to come by. Living in coastal waters, the size of your boat is only limited by the size of your wallet, and in contrast to rivers and canals, those living on the coast tend to have more of an external rather than internal perspective. For them a cruise becomes more of a voyage, and one that takes them beyond these shores.

Estuaries tend to be popular for those who want to have something bigger, and in many cases wackier! Although these too are tidal, in practice many liveaboard boats moored on estuaries spend more time on mud than water. Examples of estuary craft can vary from old lighters and barges right through to converted warships and high examples of the do-it-yourself craft which in many cases fall some way short of ever being seaworthy.

Canals remain perhaps the most popular location.

Living on a river extends the range of craft you can live on, such as this Dutch barge.

TYPE AND SIZE OF BOAT

Your preferred type of waterway will therefore to some extent limit the type and size of boat available. Another key consideration is the number of people who will be living aboard – and don't forget to include any pets – which will determine both the space required and the help available to move your boat around. A particular consideration will be whether you have, or plan to have, small children around, be they your own or grandchildren. But if you are living alone and intend to cruise around you may wish to sacrifice some space in order to have a boat that is easier to handle and look after.

Your decision on which type of boat you prefer will be driven by a number of other factors. Key considerations beyond the basic type of boat will include the amount of deck space you prefer (and any compromises this may involve with interior space) and the type of hull you will need. If you decide to go for a longer boat and know you will want to cruise a fair bit, one option at this stage will be to have a bow thruster fitted, which gives you just that bit more manoeuvrability. This is basically a small propeller fitted below the waterline which is used to push the bow to the left or right, reducing your dependence on the rudder.

Whilst narrowboats do occasionally ride coastal waters this tends to be under highly controlled conditions and even then only in short bursts. Their flat-bottomed construction makes them simply unsuitable for the task, even if some highly publicised, and ill-advised, dashes across the English Channel to the French canals are sometimes made. Equally, large river and coastal-going craft will soon find that obstacles in the way of low bridges, locks and water depth will prevent them going too far inland.

If your choice is the canals and a narrowboat then you will have a further range of options, described in more detail in the companion book *Britain's Canals: A Handbook,* which also provides more on the origins of different boat styles. Although variations exist, with these often being peculiar to individual boatyards, narrowboats fall into three broad styles, defined in terms of the profile of the boat.

The traditional 'trad' narrowboat has a small unguarded deck at the back with the cabin far enough back for the helmsman to stand inside and protect the lower half of their body from the elements. The cruiser style takes its name from the river cruiser and has large open decks at the bow and stern whilst the third type is a compromise between the two, known perhaps inevitably as the 'semi-trad'. Like the cruiser style, the hatch and rear doors are placed forward but on the semi-trad the side walls continue from the sides to give more protected seating and a modicum of shelter for the helmsman.

As you might expect, the defining feature of a narrowboat is its lack of space, and whilst this may be regarded as cosy or romantic by outsiders, that view may be open to revision if you have to live in one for any length of time. As with most things, though, this can be seen as presenting problems or a set of challenges, and later chapters in this book provide ideas on how to meet these challenges, not least those of storage and internal layout.

The obvious solution to this fundamental flaw is to opt for a wider boat and accept that this may limit your cruising options. Alternatives include wide-beam boats, generally known as barges, although this term is often inaccurately also applied to narrowboats. Barges come in their own array of types but tend to have a beam of around 12ft and much higher decks. They can be either English or Dutch in style and were originally used for navigation on larger rivers.

A barge offers more room, but they are not that manoeuvrable, and may require a crew to get around. Their size can also present problems if you move your moorings regularly, and you are limited in how far inland you can progress. As such, as a liveaboard option barges tend to be suitable if more than one person is involved and if you don't envisage moving around much.

Different types of barge were the result of different original uses, or from regional variations designed to meet specific local conditions. Often barges have their origins in boats capable of plying both the larger river navigations as well as near-coastal waters, bringing goods from inland to ocean-going ships.

Four types can be differentiated. The first of these is the Yorkshire Keel, which is distinguished by its round middle and bluff, almost flat front. These originated around Yorkshire and the Humber and owe a lot in terms of appearance to Viking longboats. The second is the Mersey Flat, characterised by its round bilge and two masts, which can be lowered or lifted out if required. The first mast tends to be about a quarter of the way down the boat with a mizzen mast on the stern deck behind the cargo.

The third type is the Trow. Originally popular along the River Severn, these come in a range of styles, typically with open holds with extra canvas bulwarks laced up to a rail. Upriver trows were mostly square-rigged, with carvel-style hulls the norm, with a vertical transom stern where the boat's name and port would be displayed proudly.

The final type of common barge is the most easily spotted today, the Thames Sailing Barge. These are characterised by flat bottoms and large tan-coloured sails, along with masts and leeboards that can be lowered. In their heyday these were typically crewed by two men or families and were highly manoeuvrable, capable of negotiating the crowded waters of the Thames as well as the creeks and docks that fed off or into the river. Originally 'swim-ended' – that is, shaped like a horizontal wedge – as time went on these became more streamlined.

A spacious cruiser stern complete with protective awning for extra safety.

Houseboat design may be functional rather than inspiring.

A variant on this theme is the lighter, which were originally used to transport goods up and down rivers. These can be up to 75ft long and are wider than a barge. The size constraints usually mean that when converted to residential use they are unpowered, since there are few places you could take them.

Other unpowered, usually permanently moored boats (although they can be towed) include the traditional houseboat. These tend not to be distinguished by their style, with a functional rectangular construction on top of a hull the norm. None of your sleek lines here – houseboats have sometimes been compared to floating ship containers converted into living space.

A further option for canal and river living is a fibreglass or GRP hull cruiser. These come in various sizes, ranging from the day boat right up to the ocean-going gin palace – often to be spotted inland on the Thames, although only as far as Oxford where the low Osney Bridge (7ft 6in headroom on a good day) tends to impede progress. Known disparagingly by some (mainly narrowboaters!) as 'plastic boats', these are cast from moulds and share many of the same problems of space with narrowboats. These boats are suitable for the Norfolk Broads and wider canals as well as most rivers and are made to standard configurations. As such they are easier to specify and fit out and, if you are buying new, tend to be available much quicker than a narrowboat.

Lighter and easier to manoeuvre (they are typically powered by diesel or petrol outboard engines), cruisers also rock around more, and for many, cruisers seem less homely and more suited to short visits or day boating. That said, a small proportion of liveaboards manage to make their homes in them.

Motor cruisers are a larger version of this type, and are usually capable of sea crossings. When negotiating the speed-restricted inland waterways, they can give the appearance of powerful vessels stuck in first or second gear. Their more natural element is the coastal marina, where many do live on board them, although year-round living tends to be less popular as life on these boats can be uncomfortable in the winter, and most such vessels are lifted out of the water out of season. But not all cruisers are clean, shiny fibreglass, and it's possible to see oddities if you look in popular mooring spots, ranging from old warships through to lifeboats and every kind of craft made from wood, steel or even concrete!

Finally, if you do not expect to move, and you have somewhere to moor, your options suddenly multiply. Certain spots, with the Thames estuary a prime example, seem to act as magnets for large and at times quite eccentric craft which, if they ever floated, are unlikely to do so again. These are often more accurately described as houses built around a hull than boats converted into homes, which brings us onto our final set of decision-making criteria.

A Humber Keel converted for life on board.

Narrowboats are the favoured vessel for many, especially on canals.

HOUSE, BOAT OR HOUSEBOAT?

Having decided where you want to be and what type of craft you prefer, a conversation needs to take place about what exactly you are trying to achieve. Is your objective to replace your house with another which just happens to be at the water's edge? If you want to cruise, then considerations of safety probably mean you want your craft to be a boat first and a home second. If you want to enjoy the pleasures of actually floating and not rule out the possibility of moving (although this would not be something you would expect to do too often), then you may wish to consider something in between: a houseboat.

Houseboats may or may not have an engine and tend to be highly functional in design, which is a polite way of saying they can be quite box-like, certainly in the UK, and may not really look like a boat at all. As their name implies, these tend to fall more into the category of floating house rather than a boat. In the eyes of the authorities houseboats tend to enjoy a more established status than other liveaboard craft, although the *quid pro quo* for this can be that they are obliged to congregate in designated spots where utilities and other basics of modern life highlighted in Chapter 1 are laid on. This state of near-permanence also reflects in the land beside them, which is often cultivated into a garden. This different status tends to set houseboats apart, a breed unto themselves and one perhaps not really 'of' the boating community – at least in some eyes. Houseboat moorings are scarce and therefore tend to be very expensive in places such as Chelsea and Little Venice.

WHERE TO START

Once you have weighed up all the various considerations discussed above and decided what sort of boat you're after, there is then the question of where to look for one. One option is to start from scratch and have a boat custom-built, or to build your own. This tends to be the most expensive way forward and the one that takes the most time, but it does mean that you are able to specify your requirements exactly. Starting from scratch tends to work best for those who have a very good idea of what it is they're after, usually because they are experienced liveaboards and have an excellent insight into their individual needs and expectations.

There is no shortage of boatbuilders willing to satisfy your needs and indeed to provide advice. Details can be gained from the boating press, with some magazines offering annual surveys of the industry, setting out areas of specific expertise. Alternatively you may choose to acquire your own hull and get involved personally in fitting it out, first having found a friendly marina with access to the tools and other kit you may need. Another option may be to convert or adapt an existing craft, which may or may not have been used previously by a liveaboard. Clearly, the further you get away from working with a clean sheet, the tighter your room for manoeuvre will become, but you may find savings in both cost and time.

If your preference is to buy off-the-peg or second-hand you have two main options, assuming you do not already have your eye on a specific craft. The first is to buy off-the-page using one of the boating magazines or one or the growing number of websites offering boats for sale, and the second is to go via a broker. Brokers tend to be based at the larger marinas and usually also have websites. These work on commission, but this is usually paid by the vendor, and going down this route does offer access to more advice and to services for checking any potential purchase out. Whilst vendors may be responsible for commissions, purchasers usually have to bear the cost of a survey, and having survey facilities on hand can help speed up the process.

Be conscious always of the maxim 'buyer beware' – as the purchaser it is your responsibility to check out what you are buying, not the seller's to point out potential problems. Unlike cars, boats do not always come with a service history or log book, although some may have some kind of proof of ownership, for example a bill of sale. Again, you may wish to make your own checks to make sure you are buying from the legal owner.

Whichever route you choose, be mindful of the golden rule: let the head rule the heart. An all-too-common tale involves potential liveaboards making the crucial decision of which boat to buy on the basis of minor details – the curtains, or the kind of stain used on the wood panelling. Even if you think you have found the boat you want – and remember this decision will inevitably involve compromise, as you will never find the perfect boat – pause before committing yourself and find time to examine and compare different boats, so you can appreciate the exact nature of the compromises you are prepared to make.

If you want to learn in more detail how to finance the purchase of a boat turn to Chapter 10, but in general terms, if you are buying a new boat the normal practice is to put down a deposit (10-20 per cent) and make staged payments at agreed points in the boat's construction. A first-stage payment might be at the point when the hull is complete, the second when the engine is fitted, and the third stage may be payable upon fitting out. This gives you the option to get a third-party opinion at different points in the boat's construction before handing over your hard-earned cash, but be aware of when these stages are coming up, as you may have to book ahead for a professional opinion and won't want to have work halted pending an inspection.

A good tip here is to work to a standard contract such as that offered by the British Marine Federation, which has been designed to protect both the boatbuilder and the customer. Be sure also that all the requirements of the EU's Recreational Craft Directive (RCD) are fulfilled, as you will not get a Boat Safety Certificate (BSC) otherwise. If you go down the route of buying a narrowboat shell to complete yourself, the supplier of the shell also has to provide an RCD Annexe 3 Certificate and you won't need to comply with the RCD requirements unless you resell the boat within five years – although you will still be obliged to get a BSC. Given that these regulations change all the time, it is worth checking that no changes have been made since publication of this book, should this be your preferred option.

Choosing a boat is only the beginning of the liveaboard story. Just as important is what you do with it afterwards. Like householders, liveaboards like to customise their space and environment and some are more diligent at maintenance than others. As such, the range of liveaboard boats is as varied as the people living on them.

Some assume the status of little palaces, following the rule of thumb that states that the amount of time spent beautifying a boat is inversely proportional to the time spent actually cruising – whatever one's initial intentions might have been. Others fall into disrepair, the ambition to 'do up' a boat being unequal to the sheer scale of the challenge. All this goes to prove that liveaboards are not such a different breed – just people.

QUESTIONS FOR CHOOSING A BOAT:

- Do you intend to cruise or will your boat be permanently moored?

- What type of waterway do you want to be on?

  Canal?
  River?
  Coastal?
  Estuary?

- What type of boat do you want?

  Narrowboat?
  Broad beam?
  River cruiser?
  Barge?
  Houseboat?
  Something different?

- What size of boat do you want?

- Will you be alone?

- Do you expect to have pets?

- What can you and your crew manage?

- What type of mooring can you afford?

- Have you considered a houseboat?

Chapter 3
Moorings

Popular notions of the waterborne equivalent of the 'freedom of the road' carry a fair degree of truth, at least if you choose the canals. So long as you pay your licence you have considerable freedom to roam the vast majority of the UK's inland waterways. The point at which reality kicks in is when you have to stop for any length of time – either at a base or moorings – and perhaps because it involves land, this is an area which has become increasingly bound up in regulations in recent years.

Liveaboards tend to fall into three broad categories. The first is what is called a 'continuous cruiser', a water nomad always on the move. Although they have no permanent mooring, this type of liveaboard is not immune to the need to stop every now and then, even if it's just for the night, and they have their own set of regulations they need to abide by.

The second group may be termed the permanently moored liveaboard. These tend to have a home mooring where they spend most, if not all their time. The third lies somewhere between the two, let's call them the semi-permanent or seasonal cruiser, who may be on the move for much of the year but moor up for the winter, not necessarily always at the same place.

CONTINUOUS CRUISERS

The regulations surrounding continuous cruising have been tightened up considerably in recent years in order to clamp down on those who sought to avoid paying mooring fees altogether. These are levied by the two main waterways authorities, British Waterways and the Environment Agency (in very rough terms the former looks after our canals and the latter our rivers), and traditionally British Waterways took a relatively benign approach to enforcing mooring regulations.

Their approach was more one of 'let's all be sensible about this' and 'if you ask we may well say yes', but increasing abuse of this attitude by a growing minority has led to the introduction of more defined rules about what they will and will not accept.

Inevitably perhaps these rules are less than clear cut and still leave a fair bit of room for flexibility. The best approach if you intend to cruise continuously probably remains to stay within the spirit of the regulations and to foster good relations with the powers that be on each patch. Mooring wardens (yes they do exist!) tend not to be quite as tenacious as traffic wardens but they have the power to be if they so choose. In practice many mooring wardens are also fellow liveaboards, which can help.

The basic definition of continuous cruising is that you are expected to be able to provide evidence of a 'genuine progressive journey', a form of words which perhaps exemplifies the 'wriggle room' British Waterways has allowed itself. Furthermore, when mooring, continuous cruisers are obliged to respect any local restrictions at popular spots and not stay in the same place for more than fourteen days.

The canny reader may spot an opportunity here to move back and forth between two spots, but on a 'genuine progressive journey' you have to be moving ever onwards like a spaceship hurtling towards the sun. Just moving a few yards doesn't count either, as you are expected to be in a different neighbourhood every fifteen days. This is another wonderfully vague choice of term and in practice is interpreted differently according to local circumstances. The onus throughout is on being sensible and keeping within the spirit of the law. The ultimate responsibility remains with the boater however, and not British Waterways, to prove that the rules are being adhered to. Equally, it should be understood that the vagueness in the definitions may work against the liveaboard in the future, with greater rigidity in interpretation more likely than any increased flexibility.

A Mooring Warden.

Continuous cruising is probably the most extreme choice for the possible liveaboard and will suit only a particular type of personality and lifestyle. Many of the potential sacrifices associated with living on board a boat, including the less tangible and more psychological aspects associated with becoming a 'floating citizen', are most profound for those who choose this option. Issues such as communications, access to services and whether or not you need to earn a living (even if a floating office makes this possible, remember that Internet access isn't yet reliable from a moving boat) are all important considerations in making this choice.

PERMANENT MOORINGS

The permanently moored enjoy greater security and more facilities – if you are lucky, maybe even an address – which come with having a base, even if this does come at the price of less freedom. For those on rivers and canals there are basically two options for long-term moorings. Either you can stay at marinas and boatyards, or you can moor bankside, with the latter subdivided into towpath and non-towpath moorings.

Marinas tend to be privately owned (although in recent years British Waterways has purchased a number of them as part of its policy of income diversification) and offer more facilities, ranging from semi-gated communities with a full range of facilities such as laundries, showers and a club house, not to mention often high levels of security including CCTV; through to bases that barely deserve to be called marinas, being little more than a spare bit of space at a boatyard.

If you decide to go down the marina route the choice is wide, and you'll be driven by where you want to be, the type of environment you are most comfortable in and the size of your wallet – for mooring in a marina is by far the most expensive option for the liveaboard. Furthermore, if you do decide to make a marina your home, you need to check first whether this is something that is encouraged, as some marinas are keener than others on having permanent residents. Some marinas explicitly ban residential moorings, whilst others have what may be termed a flexible approach, with individuals judged on a case-by-case basis.

Another consideration is whether you expect to be doing a lot of work to your boat. Few marina owners are happy when their facility begins to look like a construction site. In these cases a mooring attached to a boatyard is the better option, as not only do you have access to professional expertise, but boatyards are also better equipped to take deliveries of materials.

Finally, one recent development has been the sale of leasehold moorings (typically for thirty years) so that when a boat is sold its mooring can go with it. Whilst this does provide extra security it also comes with some risk attached. How do you know that the marina will remain in its current ownership for the duration of your lease? Also, if you ever want to sell your boat, is there any guarantee that the new owner will also want to live in the marina?

Non-towpath or offside bankside mooring tends to be made available either by marinas, boatyards or cruising clubs. There are over 100 cruising clubs in the UK, grouped together under the umbrella of the Association of Waterways Cruising Clubs (see Learn More and Links), with many of them offering a berth to the liveaboard as well as an instant community to become part of.

Offside mooring is also possible by buying or renting a strip of private land alongside a waterway, and although these are not cheap, they can be quite cost-effective compared with the alternatives, and especially if you are looking to moor in a city centre. Be warned though – good spots are usually snapped up as soon as they become available, and if you rely on picking one up through an advert you are likely to be disappointed. Instead you need to hook into the boating grapevine, with mooring wardens, other liveaboards and boatyard owners all good sources of information.

It is not possible simply to buy a strip of land and declare it a mooring, but that's not to say you cannot buy a strip of land and have it approved as a mooring. In the case of canals the water is 'owned' by British Waterways, whereas purchase of a strip of land alongside a river does bring with it certain riparian rights including owning the water to the centre of the river. If you are looking to create a coastal mooring then you will need to gain permission from the Crown Estate.

Both British Waterways and the Environment Agency like to pass approval on potential sites and will charge you for the privilege, in the case of the former typically at half the rate of equivalent local moorings. The Environment Agency will also wish to ensure that a possible mooring will not represent a hazard in the event of a flood. The authorities also reserve the right to refuse you mooring status, for example if you are too close to a bridge or a lock or are likely to present a navigational hazard. Once again, common sense tends to prevail, although recent trends suggest that the authorities are becoming more begrudging in their approval of such moorings.

Until recently towpath moorings have been the most straightforward option for the liveaboard, assuming of course that this is permitted in the spot you have your eye on. On one level these offer the convenience of being able to access 'the system' easily, as well as being less expensive than the alternative, but they are likely to be less well endowed with facilities than, say, a marina. On the canals and rivers, towpath moorings are controlled by the relevant authorities, and the reality has been that towpath moorings have been much easier to obtain on canals than they are on rivers. That said, these moorings are the subject of the laws of supply and demand. Until recently British Waterways operated on a 'waiting list' principle. If you wanted a place on one of their designated moorings you put your name down and waited until a suitable opportunity came up.

This approach had the virtue of equality, but it did mean that you could wait forever to get your ideal spot, and would have to do a fair bit of moving around until your number came up. But not even its staunchest supporters would suggest that this approach was efficient. Applicants may pass long, empty stretches at their preferred sites every day only to be told that these were 'reserved'. For better or worse, economic pressures from elsewhere have recently led British Waterways to replace this approach with another, altogether more stark, policy of auctioning places off to the highest bidder when they become available via sealed bids.

A boat, but not afloat!

A tidal mooring, complete with a gangway that rises with the tide.

It now seems that the thickness of a potential moorer's wallet will become the key factor in deciding whether or not they gain the mooring they desire, a move that has angered many. To be fair to British Waterways, their financial problems have come about through no fault of their own, and as experience elsewhere has shown, land always carries a value and perhaps they'd be foolish not to realise it. But all that aside, it does seem a shame that another part of the democratic ethos of the canals has fallen by the wayside.

At the same time there seems to have been a mood shift in the recent past away from online moorings which are felt to have become too congested in certain places – a consideration when other users are required to slow down past moored boats. Increasingly, liveaboards are being encouraged through force of circumstance to seek either a non-towpath base or locations that are off the beaten track, such as disused arms or basins.

But at whatever cost it comes, a permanent bankside mooring does offer the opportunity for that most innocent of an Englishman's pleasures: his garden. Being closer to nature tends to bring out the gardener in even the least green-fingered boater, and rare is the liveaboard who doesn't make at least some attempt to grow some of their own food (even if it's just a few herbs) or to adorn their boat with flowerpots. A rough rule of thumb suggests that the more pots a boat has, the less it travels, with the pots offering both tangible and intangible evidence of roots having been laid down.

This gardening instinct is less easy to satisfy in a marina, probably because boats are more likely to be moored alongside pontoons, or because there is less sense of permanence in a marina. Bankside

Up the creek?

mooring does offer this opportunity, even if it is curtailed somewhat if you choose a towpath mooring.

Towpath moorings tend to be controlled by the relevant authority and although liveaboards tend to be welcome (although it's worth checking first), the corollary to this is that any form of 'colonisation' of the towpath, whether it be a few grow-bags, a lockable storage chest or even leaving a wheelbarrow or bike out, tends to be discouraged, with purges (depending upon how zealous local officials might be) accompanied by threatened sanctions a not infrequent occurrence. Generally speaking, tolerance levels in this area have fallen in recent years, and although this may mean a tidier towpath, it has come at the price of a smaller number of informal communities existing alongside them.

This tendency can be seen as part of a wider gentrification of the waterways in the last decade or so. As in other spheres of life, as the users of the waterways have become gradually more affluent, they have also become more protective and perhaps less tolerant of features of the waterways which, although they may have been there for years, are in their eyes responsible for 'spoiling the neighbourhood'. As such, the traditional 'water gypsy' is not always seen as welcome!

Finally on the issue of canalside moorings, before selecting a location it is worth checking some of the things you cannot see, such as the depth of the water and whether the bed is regularly dredged. How often is the bankside vegetation cut? Other issues worth thinking about include how easy it might be to dispose of rubbish and your access to sanitary facilities. On all these issues, the best source of information by far is people who are already in the vicinity.

Marina moorings complete with electrical hook-ups.

Permanent riverside moorings are much harder to come by than those on the canals and potential liveaboards planning to live by a river have to secure their berth before they buy their boat. It has been estimated that a boat roughly triples in value if it has a permanent residential mooring, so long as the tenure is for at least ten years. These do not come cheap however, and like everything the more desirable it is the more it will cost, with the best running into thousands of pounds a year. Sites in the middle of London, for example, are the subject of NHS-style waiting lists, only there is no guarantee that you will ever get to the top.

That said there can be little doubt that living on board a boat remains an 'alternative' option for many – at least on most of our inland waterways, though this is probably less true on our coasts. As a result, plenty of unconventional communities or individual moorings still exist to provide some colour to the liveaboard scene.

One example of this is the run of 'Agenda 21' moorings outside Oxford on the South Oxford Canal. These are five designated zones where traditional boating communities are allowed to moor long term, the term 'Agenda 21' referring to an EU Directive encouraging the preservation of traditional lifestyles.

Finally, tidal moorings come with their own complexities and the best source of information on these is the Yacht Harbour Association (see Learn More and Links). In short, tidal moorings tend to fall into classifications which indicate how easy they are to get away from. A mud berth is a mooring that dries out when the tide recedes, leaving your boat sitting on mud, which can make access difficult if you are not tied up to a jetty and can bring with it related problems, not least the smell of the mud.

Some tidal moorings may be classified as +/- 2 hours HW, meaning that you can move your boat two hours either side of high water. Others may be termed Half Tide moorings, whereby your boat can be moved for half the tide, or All States of Tide, which is self-explanatory. Boats will rise and fall with the tide. Flat-bottomed boats need to sit on bearers so the incoming water can get underneath the boat or it may stay down as a vacuum forms between the bottom of the boat and the mud below. At low tide such boats may become inaccessible.

SEMI-PERMANENT MOORINGS

Semi-permanent moorings can offer a potential 'win-win' to both land owners and those whose liveaboard status may vary with the seasons. If you are a semi-permanent cruiser, i.e. out on the water on a 'continuous voyage' for part of the year but holed up on dry land for the rest of the year – an increasingly popular option amongst retired people who may have a property abroad or swapped their family home for a more convenient flat – then you still need somewhere to leave your boat in the off season, exactly the time that boatyards are keen to generate some extra income and when less traffic means its possible to juggle more boats in the same space. A useful tip is that British Waterways sometimes provides winter moorings from October to March using summer visitor moorings and it is normally worth checking to see if there any available in your area. Another option for this breed is to own a property which has its own water-frontage, although remember that the authorities will need to sanction its use as a mooring (see above).

The advice given above represents the official line. However, as may be becoming clear by now, within this there does remain some room for what might be called 'interpretation' on the ground. Although often demonised, the waterways authorities exist to serve their customers and their representatives on the ground may often take a more pragmatic view of what is and is not acceptable in a particular locality. Although they would never admit it, it is not unknown for them to turn the occasional blind eye to situations which may have existed for years or are doing no one any real harm. This cannot be relied upon however and it is fair to say that regulations have been more firmly enforced in recent years. That said, our waterways and coasts represent many thousands of miles with all sorts of nooks and crannies capable of harbouring the whole range of life afloat!

QUESTIONS FOR MOORINGS:

- Do you need a permanent base?

- Are you a continuous cruiser, someone needing a permanent mooring, or a semi-permanent mooring?

- What range of facilities do you value most?

- Where's the nearest water point?

- If you are considering a bankside mooring consider how the immediate vicinity may change with the seasons – will it get muddy or flood for instance?

- If there are existing liveaboards where you are considering mooring, talk to them and ask them about the good and bad things about living there.

- How close are the shops and other non-immediate facilities?

- Will you want access to other transport? What is public transport like? Is there somewhere to leave a car/motorbike/bike safely if need be?

Chapter 4
Engines

Whether you intend to cruise or not, the one thing you cannot do without as a liveaboard is an engine. Your engine is more than a simple means of propulsion. Unless you have a permanent mooring with mains power, your engine will be your main source of energy, and as such, lies at the heart of your life-support system. It's surprising, therefore, how often engines are taken for granted, especially when looking round a potential liveaboard craft when it's all too easy to get caught up in other things such as living space and decoration.

There are a number of things to take into consideration when it comes to engines including their size and type, location, the space they take up, their efficiency and their noise. At its most basic level decisions about your engine will probably involve some level of compromise between image and practicality. You may come to curse that brass-piped beauty you saw on display in the marina when you have to live with it.

Let's start with the most practical consideration for a liveaboard: space. Certain boat styles will dictate where the engine is located. A cruiser-style narrowboat, for example, will have its engine under the deck, out of the living area and still nicely convenient to service and repair – so long as it isn't cold and wet outside. A 'trad' narrowboat, on the other hand, requires the engine to be in what would otherwise be living space. Some vintage-style engines may need as much as a 2m-long separate engine room inside the boat, a sizeable proportion of the total available, and although it may be possible to use some of this space as a utility or drying area, remember that the space will invariably be dirty and smell of diesel.

This is when it is important to remember the dual uses of the engine, since even when you are not moving an engine would typically have to run for 2-3 hours a day to top up the cabin batteries and heat up water if you don't have a separate boiler. An inboard engine will generate not only power but also a lot of vibration and noise during this time, to say nothing of the fumes. For these reasons excellent ventilation and probably sound-proofing are also essential for the liveaboard to consider.

Another important consideration when running an engine is your neighbours, be they fellow boaters or people living in nearby houses. Many areas have local by-laws restricting the running of engines to certain times of day, and signs requesting considerate use are becoming more familiar. Whether or not you run your engine in or out of gear is a matter of personal preference. Some schools of thought suggest an engine will run cooler when in gear and under a working load, but remember that the wash may affect boats moored in the immediate vicinity and local wildlife, and perhaps most important of all, tends to erode the bank. Finally, running an engine in gear is also considerably noisier.

Before considering the relative merits of different types of engine it is worth bearing in mind their origins. The fact is that most marine engines are in fact adaptations of automotive or industrial engines; very few are designed specifically for marine use. This is significant because an automotive or industrial engine is built to do a very different job from a marine engine, with an emphasis on delivering power at higher revolutions per minute through the use of gearboxes. A boat, on the other hand, needs an engine which will provide strong, low-speed power at the propeller, which means that a marinised engine needs detuning and low gearing to convert high-speed power into low-speed torque. Add to this the need to protect the engine from water and to configure it in such a way that it is easily accessible (since, for obvious reasons, it is usually not possible to get underneath a marine engine) and one can see why marinised conventional engines usually represent a compromise. The one big advantage of using marinised car or industrial engines, however, is that they do benefit from a worldwide distribution network for spares.

Marine engines offer compromises in other areas also. The fact that they are required to push their burden through water rather than through air adds complications to the balance between power and performance. At the optimum power for a certain hull shape, adding more power will not produce more performance, since increasing power will also increase the hydraulic forces acting against the boat, and hence slow it down. At optimum power the boat is supported by a wave crest at the bow and another at the stern. Add more power and the aft crest moves down to the stern, which has the effect of making the boat want to move uphill.

A Shire engine installation.

When it comes to canal boats there are basically two families of engine to choose between. The first is the vintage type, typically slow-revving and delivering high torque, which means these need a large propeller and, in turn, a deeper draft boat. This may be an issue if you intend to live mainly on canals. They are also usually cooled by raw water, which does mean that you have to keep the mud box clean to prevent overheating.

The advantage of this type of engine is their looks, and a well-maintained vintage engine can be a thing of beauty to those of a certain disposition. They also typically have a distinctive sound all of their own, a sort of deep-toned chug which summons up memories of fairgrounds. Traditional names such as Lister, Petter, Gardner, Enfield and Russell Newbury dominate this sector and having a certain type of engine can be a good ice-breaker when meeting new people on the canals.

The other main family of engine is the modern type, usually based on Japanese industrial designs. These would typically be the type of engine offered to a potential liveaboard buying a new boat. Higher-revving, these require a smaller propeller, are quieter, smoother-running and can power three alternators to charge an engine battery,

Above: *A Beta engine installation.*
(Courtesy Kingsground Narrowboats)

Right: *A boxed-in super-silent engine.*

a 12V supply for the marine systems, and a 240V domestic system (see Chapter 6 for more on electrics). Names here include companies such as Barras Shire, Beta and Vetus. There are also still a number of BMC- and Ford-based engines in use. These engines tend to be keel-cooled with a tank built into the swim so that the engine is cooled by transferring heat into the canal or river.

When it comes to what size and make of engine to choose it's best to listen to advice. If you are having a new boat built for you, your boatyard will have its own opinions on which is best, notably in terms of reliability as they will not want you coming back all the time with problems while it is still under warranty. When listening to recommendations on size it is always worth asking what it would cost to have the next size up – you may find it is only a marginal cost for a benefit you will appreciate for years.

Inevitably perhaps, choosing your engine involves yet a further compromise – here between image and practicality. Either type will do the job but if your main concern is practicality, the more modern engines are probably the best bet. Being higher-revving means that the alternator doesn't have to be geared up so much and some have a cooling system fitted with more than one thermostat, which means that the contents of the water tank heats up more quickly via a califorier heating coil.

Most boat engines are fitted towards the bottom of the hull (although not always) and towards the stern. The gearbox allows a simple selection choice of forward, neutral and reverse, whilst also reducing the revolutions of the propeller shaft by around a factor of two in order to improve efficiency. If the engine is fitted on a flexible mounting, which is done to reduce vibration, then the propeller shaft will be connected via a flexible coupling. The shaft then passes through the hull to the propeller via a stern gland which needs to be regularly greased and the packing adjusted in order to prevent leakage back into the engine compartment.

A key consideration with engines is their cooling. The sheer amount of work an engine is required to do means that an engine will overheat if there is no system for cooling it. This is achieved either through an air- or water-cooling system. Air-cooling systems are very straightforward, involving a duct and a fan and so long as both remain in working order the engine should remain cool – although some excess heat should still be expected to emanate from the engine (in fact, most cooling systems only remove about a third of the heat generated). Although cheap and simple, air-cooling systems do have the disadvantage of being noisy.

Simple water-cooled systems use the principle of drawing in water, channelling it through the cylinder block and head, round the exhaust manifold and then back into the river or canal. Whilst much quieter than an air-cooled system, this approach has its own disadvantages. Water drawn into the system inevitably includes impurities and these can accumulate in the pipes. The solution is to use thermostat-controlled heat-exchanging technology, in which fresh water is passed through the engine, and the pipes of hot fresh water are then cooled by contact with cold canal water.

It is worth pausing to consider the work that you expect an engine to do for you. Anyone who's ever tried to turn an engine manually to see how much power they can generate will soon realise the value of an efficient machine, and also, critically, of a good alternator – the device which converts the mechanical energy created by the engine into electrical energy. Alternators take a lot of power out of an engine, so it's worth considering just how many electrical devices you want to run off it. Again, this subject is covered in more detail later on. This purpose of the engine is a good reason why few liveaboards choose a river cruiser as their home, as these tend to be powered by outboard engines and need a separate generator to do all the work that an inboard engine would also do for you.

Access to the engine has already been touched upon and is a key factor. Engines need to be easy to reach, as there are few things worse than having to take your furniture apart every time you want to carry out some basic maintenance, and such work is part of the regular routine of any liveaboard (see Chapter 8). The engine and the gearbox both need to be within easy reach, as running repairs such as changing the fuel filters and adjusting or replacing the alternator belts are both regular jobs.

All the above engines are diesel-fuelled and there are a number of good reasons for this. Not only is petrol dangerous to store and handle, it also tends to need an electrical ignition system and these often find it hard to cope with exposure to damp conditions. It is also more expensive, even after the planned rises in the cost of red diesel (and even its possible abolition) are taken into account. Petrol does have a place in powering marine engines however, although this tends to be confined to outboard motors for smaller, lighter craft. Most boaters are stuck with the smellier and noisier alternative.

There are other types of engine but these are of curiosity value only to the liveaboard, with examples including electric, steam and semi-diesel engines. Electric engines have the advantage of being cheap and easy to operate, although they are practical only for very light boats. Other options of more interest include hydraulic drives, which offer more freedom on the critical question of where to locate the engine and can be worth considering.

QUESTIONS FOR ENGINES:

- Inside or outside – where would you prefer the engine to be?

- Old or new? Do you want a thing of beauty which will need more maintenance (and might this even be a pleasure for you?) or do you want something more practical?

- If you are buying new consider going to the next size up, as it may only be a marginal extra cost for a significant benefit over time.

- Which cooling system – air or water?

- Make sure you can get at your engine to conduct regular maintenance.

Chapter 5
Lifestyle and Layout

The ideal layout of a liveaboard boat needs to reflect its occupants' lifestyle, and as everyone's lifestyle is different, so that ideal will also be different. The problem is that there's only a finite number of things you can do in the restricted space offered by a boat, and much of that is taken up by essentials such as the engine and your life-support mechanisms, without which it's impossible to have any lifestyle at all!

The liveaboard therefore quickly learns a new respect for space if they are not to make too many compromises to their old lifestyle and thus defeat the point of becoming a liveaboard in the first place. And here lies the crux. Many of those seeking to become a liveaboard do so because they are looking for a shift in their lifestyle – it is after all a fairly radical decision. As such, 'normal' determinants of lifestyle shouldn't be allowed to dictate one's lifestyle afloat, and priorities will inevitably change. Those who try to make the transition thinking they will simply replicate how they lived onshore, albeit perhaps scaled down a little, are almost certainly condemning themselves to failure. A fresh mindset is needed; one that relishes the opportunities and freedoms that living aboard offers, rather than fights it.

To return to the theme of space. Those used to living in a house with a garden, an attic and maybe even a junk room can become blasé about space – which a liveaboard can never do. Before opting to become a liveaboard, it can be useful to look around your house and redefine what you regard as essential items. Thinking again of that point about fresh opportunities, moving onto a boat may represent the ultimate chance to de-clutter your life, to ask not 'what do I want?' but instead ask 'what do I need?' with the line between luxury and necessity becoming much starker.

In practical terms a key consideration here is practicality, usually a delicate balance between size, utility, whether any power is required to make it function (and if so how much) and ease of storage. Even items you may currently regard as basics, such as a vacuum cleaner or an ironing board, may be called into question, and that's long before you get onto thinking about the microwave, the coffee-grinder and the bread-maker.

This is where considerations of each individuals' lifestyle come into play. If your life isn't worth living without freshly baked bread, what are you prepared to trade in order to get it? A good place to start is a cold analysis of what you really do need in order to function. Those who are still working and need to be smartly turned out every day may place a higher value on an ironing board and hanging wardrobe space – and don't forget that an electric iron is a very high consumer of electricity.

If you are semi-retired or intend to telecommute from your boat, or indeed have become a 'silver surfer' who finds technology the ideal way to keep in touch with children and grandchildren, then some kind of office with a computer will be high up on your list of priorities, as well a means of communicating with the outside world (discussed in more detail below). Do you like to entertain? Do you have pets? Do you play a musical instrument? All these are considerations.

BOAT LAYOUT BASICS

With the exception of houseboats and early narrowboats, water craft are not really designed to be lived on all year round, and indeed, those who originally lived on working narrowboats had to manage with a living space barely larger than a decent-sized kennel. This is not to say that creating a desirable living space isn't possible; in fact there is now plenty of knowledge available on what does and doesn't work on boats (see 'Learn More and Links'), which, when combined with further intelligence gleaned from the caravan world, allows the potential liveaboard to construct pretty much whatever they want. What it does mean, however, is that it is something you have to work at to achieve.

For reasons explored elsewhere in this book, narrowboats tend to be the most popular vessels for the potential liveaboard, and although many of the hints and tips outlined apply equally to other types of craft, the rest of this chapter will focus on them. The choice of craft has already been covered in Chapter 2, but to this should be added a mention of not only a boat's interior space, but also its exterior.

Decks and outside storage need to be factored into any decisions – having a secure cratch cover for example may mean that what may previously have been considered 'dead' space may be converted into 'live' storage, although with a diminished sense of security. Decks and roofs can also be used to store awkward items such as bikes or even small mopeds or garden furniture. Equally, if you are not constrained by the heights of bridges it may be possible to add extra 'stories', with some houseboats having a second floor and larger river craft more than one deck level.

Assuming you have decided on what type of boat you want and have your hull and insulation sorted out (for more on this, see Chapter 7) your next decision is probably the interior finish. There are basically three options for wall covering: wood, paper or fabric, although not all these options may be available on a fibreglass or GRP cruiser.

Wood has the advantage of offering a warm feel and traditional look as well as a wide range of finishes, from light oak or ash to the darker mahogany or teak, with the lighter shades tending to be less claustrophobic. Wood panelling may be tongue-and-groove or veneered onto ply or blockboard, with hardwood used for detailing, or for window and door surrounds. An alternative is to use plain pine, although this tends to be less popular these days, perhaps because it darkens with age and can be a fire hazard near a chimney or stove.

Walls can also be finished with fabric, in a variety of styles. The walls can either be completely finished in this way, or just from the gunwale up, or one can carpet the walls from the gunwale down, which adds to the insulation of the boat and has the added advantage of being cheap. Walls may also be painted or papered, although this tends to be more common in houseboats. Similar options exist for ceilings.

When it comes to floor coverings there are four main options. Carpet tiles are a popular choice, being hard-wearing and easy to replace – although it is always a good tip to buy extras when you first fit them, as getting exact replacements afterwards is not always as easy as you might expect. Fitted carpets need to be laid by a professional and, as is often the way, you get what you pay for. There will be clear paths through the boat which will be trodden much more frequently than others and so hardiness will be important, as will ease of cleaning – it will not always be possible to change into carpet slippers every time you need to walk through. It is also worth fitting insulation under carpets, since after all, your floor level is below the waterline.

Wooden floors are also favoured for their durability and general utility and are an especially good idea if you have a dog. They can stain if allowed to stay wet, however, and be damaged by heavier types of footwear (and heels) as well as having the potential to get extremely slippery when wet. Floor tiles are also an option. They can be cold first thing in the morning to bare feet though, and a rug secured with non-slip tape is highly recommended. Finally, vinyl flooring has its place in the galley and bathroom areas, and again a non-slip variety is a good idea. These have the virtue of cleaning easily and being extremely hard-wearing.

Now you have the basic interior decided, you need to think about how to split it up into different rooms. In theory you can divide your space however you want to, but inevitably there are practical constraints, some of which are touched on elsewhere, such as the position of the engine, location of the boiler and where water and possibly a waste tank may go. On top of these there are more psychological considerations. It is likely that you will want to have the main living area near the front, so that passengers can appreciate the view when you're moving, and different people will have different opinions on the ideal proximity between the sleeping area and the bathroom. Whilst on the subject of bathrooms and toilets, most will also prefer to keep these away from the galley area.

When considering your ideal layout also think about traffic. Do you want your bedroom to be part of a main thoroughfare? It may be a good idea to avoid any sharp corners for those moments when you have to rush through the boat from one end to the other. If your previous experience of a boat has been a holiday hire, do not assume that what works for a week or two will work as well all year round – it won't. Your tolerance levels will change and there will be things you do and items you need if you are living aboard that you will actively avoid when you are on holiday, such as a decent set of tools.

Holiday and liveaboard craft will share the same separate living zones, even if the priority attached to each of them may vary. These are:

- Galley and Dining Area
- Sleeping Area
- Bathroom
- Living Area

Each of these is considered in turn below, along with some thoughts on an office area and general thoughts on storage, furnishings, lighting and ventilation. This chapter then ends by exploring the merits and challenges of fitting out a boat, along with some outline costs.

GALLEY AND DINING AREA

A well-planned galley should be easy to prepare food in, with everything you need to hand. It is not a good idea to have to stand in a walkway when using the sink or the stove, and for this reason an L-shaped galley is a popular idea. In a well-designed galley there should be adequate room for a cooker, oven, grill, fridge, sink/drainer and food storage. Remember, when cruising away from access to supermarkets you need a good supply of fresh food and tinned food to fall back on, especially dried milk.

A typical narrowboat galley.

Opposite above: *Waking up in your own floating palace is a dream for many.*

Opposite below: *Are you the social type, who might want to live on a marina?*

There's no denying that the liveaboard life offers opportunities for alternative ways of doing things.

Welcome aboard!

It won't always be summer!

Above left: *A highly unusual diesel-fired oven.*

Above right: *Environmentally friendly detergents are a must when living aboard.*

Left: *A 12 volt fridge showing the capacity you might expect on board.*

Below: *A foldaway table can create valuable space.*

Somewhere, a decision needs to be made on which domestic appliances are really necessary, taking into account the demands placed on electricity elsewhere. Boiled water and toast will tend to be delivered via the hob whilst appliances such as microwaves and dishwashers begin to fall into the realms of luxury items, the latter not least because of the demands it will also place upon your limited water supply.

If you feel the need to cook on a maritime Aga, weight considerations will demand that this goes near the centre of the boat, thereby dictating many of your layout decisions. Cookers can be stand-alone or built-in, and like most domestic versions, can include an eye-level grill or have the oven and hob as separate. Assuming that you are not always going to be close to an electricity hook-up, fridges and freezers (the latter are useful if you are living aboard, but do consume a lot of electricity) really need to be as close to the batteries as possible, which in turn tends to lead to the galley area being towards the rear of the boat, nearer to the engine.

Where the galley is sited will most likely determine the position of the eating area. Whilst this may be a separate area it is more likely that it will be incorporated into the main living area, with this space serving a dual purpose. Equally, as already mentioned, you are unlikely to want to locate your toilets near the galley and already it can be seen how one decision tends to inform the next when it comes to layout design. The reality is that some form of open-plan layout will tend to result, with clever design ideas, such as storage areas or bookshelves acting as internal walls, used to break up areas. Not only is open-plan more efficient, but it also makes your interior less claustrophobic.

On the subject of storage, it is vital to have somewhere to store your food which combines accessibility with tidiness. This is another area where caravan design has had an influence on boats, and their innovative and effective ideas, such as shelves which pull out vertically rather than horizontally to save space, can be copied. Storage needs to be clever, with no space left unused. Check out how corners are used in any design and look out for good ways to hang items you will need regularly, but not in a way that will allow them to fall should you have a slight altercation with the side of a lock wall or another boat! Kitchen units can be of standard domestic design, with much the same opportunities to add features through design and tiling that you would have in a house.

BATHROOM

Bathrooms represent a good example of the different standards that may be applied to a holiday and a liveaboard boat. They are also an area where fittings need to be slightly different from the standard domestic issue. Some kind of shower or sit-in bath is likely to be desirable, as is somewhere to wash clothes, or at least to dry them on those wet autumn days when you can't let them dry in the breeze (although a bath does offer the potential to act both as somewhere to wash clothes and somewhere convenient to hang them while they dry). Small baths are by no means out of the question, but your options here are determined by the size of your water tank and water heating capacity.

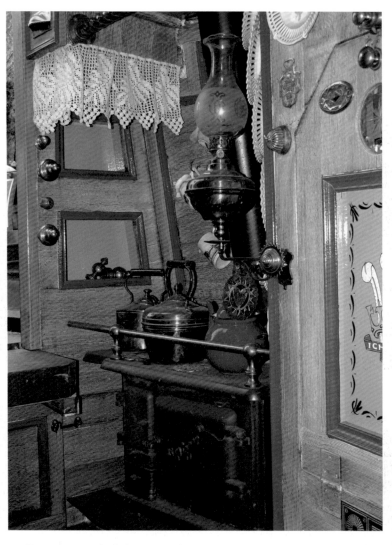

Narrowboats typically have a premium on space.

Opposite above: *Rivers offer one alternative as a waterway.*

Opposite below: *Dallas comes to the river.*

Above left: *A full shower.*

Above right: *Clever design can allow for a decent bathroom area.*

Vanity units on a boat tend to be built to take into account the limited space, whilst Chapter 7 provides more details on toilet options. The waste tank also needs to be as close to the centre of the boat as possible, otherwise the boat will list noticeably to one side as it fills, offering a rather obvious advertisement as to the state of your tank for anyone observant enough to notice!

As a liveaboard you will also want to think through your fresh water capacity if you are not to be constantly refilling your tank. Equally, if your water is going to stay around longer you may wish to consider a separate supply for drinking water or, as a minimum, some kind of filter. Grey water from the bath or shower usually has to be pumped out of the boat as it is below the waterline.

SLEEPING AREA

Sleeping accommodation is a further area where attitudes will change if you are spending more than a week or two on board. You will almost certainly prefer a permanent bed to one which you have to assemble every night and scrabble around to find the bedclothes for. Sleeping bags are okay but they are not a long-term solution.

If you are going to live aboard a narrowboat a permanent bed will have to run fore-and-aft, especially if you happen to be over 5ft 10in tall! Other types of bed, for example fold-out bunks (especially good for small children) and tables that convert into a bed using Desmo legs, should not be ruled out – but reserved for guests! The boatman's cabin is a favourite area for guest accommodation. When planning your boat layout also check that the bed is actually long enough, as it has not been unknown for boats to be sold because the 6ft owner made the mistake of buying a boat with a 5ft 6in bed.

Above: *This office area actually converts into a bunk bed for guests.*

Left: *Bunks are a popular option.*

Below: *A pull-out can give good temporary extra width for a bed.*

The difference between a wide and narrow beam can be startling when seen side-by-side.

Inner-city living – liveaboard style!

Palatial living.

A typical wide-beam boat in a city mooring.

The sleeping area is one that offers plenty of potential for ingenuity, especially for storage. The space under the bed is one such area, although this can be used for the water or toilet pump-out tank (even if you wouldn't want to be reminded too often if it was the latter!). Storage above the bed is also a possibility, although care needs to be taken that this does not become a magnet for the top of your head every morning. Whether this is practical will depend on other factors such as the shape of the walls (most of them slope) and whether or not there is a window – most people like to have a window in the sleeping area.

A bed does need to have air circulating under it if the mattress is not to become mouldy, as many caravan owners will testify. There also needs to be ventilation in the sleeping area. Finally, a built-in bedside light or ceiling spotlight with a separate switch would be normal in this area.

LIVING AREA

Somewhere to relax and maybe entertain in is an essential component of the liveaboard life. This is your retreat and it needs to be a pleasant, comfortable and above all practical space. It is here that you will locate most of your creature comforts such as entertainment systems, books and whatever – quite literally – floats your boat pastime-wise. It should not be an afterthought, just the space left over when you've fitted everything else in; claustrophobic, certainly if you wish to avoid cabin fever; or untidy, as clutter too can contribute not only to accidents (that book or piece of equipment carelessly stowed) but considerable frustration when you need to find something.

Like a living room in a house, the configuration of this retreat may well be driven by whether or not you have a TV, although in a boat it is likely that this will be considerably more modest than many of the monsters now found in many people's homes. At least one comfortable chair is desirable if you have the space, and if you are clever this may be convertible into a guest bed also.

As already mentioned, the living area may also double up as the eating area and if so a collapsible table, usually hinged from the side of the boat, may be a good idea to create a change in feel. Entertainment systems such as the TV and music are normally housed in a built-in cupboard for their security and protection during the day, and they can 'come out to play' in the evening. For this reason a flat screen TV is also a good idea.

Above: *The living area within a cruiser – which may be even more cramped than a narrowboat.*

Left: *An economical use of space for your entertainment system. (Courtesy Kingsground Narrowboats)*

If you have opted to have a stove (see Chapter 7) then this too will most likely be in the living area, and towards the front of the boat so that smoke from the chimney does not blow into the helmsman's eyes. Living areas also tend to be towards the front of the boat for the reasons touched upon above and because they are then further away from the engine and therefore quieter when you have to recharge the batteries. Should this be the case, it is also likely to be near the steps leading up to the foredeck, the space behind which offers a convenient place to locate outdoor shoes.

Overcrowding can be a problem.

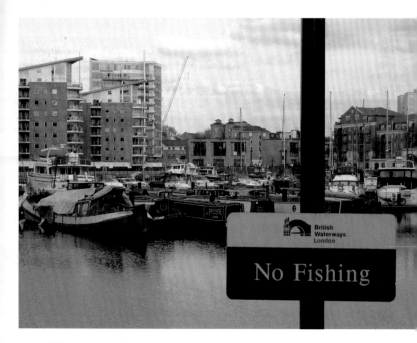

Different types of boat side-by-side.

Agenda 21 moorings in South Oxford.

A well-tended towpath mooring.

The living area is also where you are probably going to have your shelving for books, DVDs and so on, and all those knick-knacks that make a boat a home. These will have to have a lip or bar on them to stop them tumbling out at the earliest opportunity and there is plenty of scope for inventiveness for where you locate them. Have a look at what other people have done before committing yourself – an excellent rule to apply throughout this chapter, with the two main boat shows held at Crick, Northamptonshire in late May and the IWA's annual event held at various locations over August Bank Holiday weekend both good places to start.

OFFICE SPACE

Mention has already been made of the possibility of an office space on board a boat. In reality, with laptops it is less the computer itself that takes up the space than all the other paper-based paraphernalia that goes with a modern office, ranging from filing to a printer (top feed printers have a smaller footprint but for some reason are becoming increasingly hard to find).

An elegant solution to the storage problem. (Courtesy Kingsground Narrowboats)

These steps also act as storage beneath.

The reality, though, is that for better or worse, most lifestyles have begun to incorporate the use of a computer and, love or loathe them, they do offer an excellent way to keep in touch with people when deprived of landline phones. That said, gaining the functionality most homeowners now take for granted isn't easy, with broadband access speeds very much the exception rather than the rule.

Internet access tends to be achieved via a mobile phone using GPRS, a slow and expensive option and one that is likely to make you curse email attachments. At the time of writing some users have migrated to using 3G cards on their mobiles, although this remains expensive and initial reports suggest extremely patchy coverage which drops back to GPRS quality at the first opportunity. A further option is to install a satellite link, although again you would need to have a high usage to justify the cost – as well as a lot of patience!

The reality is that most liveaboards who need to access the Internet at broadband speeds either do it using Wi-Fi hotspots, with many pubs and marinas beginning to cotton onto the commercial potential of offering this, or by accessing a connection at a local library or cybercafé, which can cost around £5 per hour.

Other communications pose similar problems. While it is possible to have a landline telephone if you are permanently moored, the only realistic option if you are on the move is a mobile phone. This is a considerable improvement on only a few years ago when keeping in touch meant studying OS maps for the public telephone symbol. Mobile reception inside a boat (especially if it is metal) tends to be unreliable though, which can be inconvenient if the weather's bad as you have no other choice other than to go outside.

It's a similar story when it comes to television and if you can't live without the goggle box then you will need an external aerial (the same is true for radios), although some boaters opt for having a TV and DVD/video and eschew live TV. Once again, it depends on preferred lifestyle.

STORAGE

Storage has been mentioned more than once in this chapter and its importance should not be underestimated. The watchword here is ingenuity. Wherever there is a gap consider whether it could be used to store something, especially if it is a hidden gap – but within reason, as you are also trying to avoid a cluttered look.

A typical narrowboat mooring.

A Broads cruiser on an inner-city mooring.

Of course, not everyone has a mooring!

A bike is a good idea when your mooring is a distance from the shops.

A good example of this is the engine compartment, which can be used for storing tools, as can other under-floor storage, such as might be available under the foredeck, depending on the location of your water tank. Under-gunwale storage is also often utilised. Clips can also be used to great effect to secure items to walls and ceilings and if you have the space available, think what you might be able to achieve by raising your bed by a foot or so (although remember the need to keep an air flow going).

Cupboard space is another area, with very few liveaboards really needing a full-length cupboard, with a rail halfway down being far more useful. On this subject, also be sure to use the space around your boiler as an airing cupboard or even drying space, or alternatively use the engine room for the latter if you have an internal engine. Under-seat storage is a must and cupboard space needs to have adjustable shelves to fully utilise the space on offer.

Think of storage in terms of what you want to store. Clothes storage will require different standards than coal for example, and you will want to keep clean and dirty clothes separate. Small items may need stackable containers and most DIY chains offer a range of ingenious storage solutions, as do some of the plastics specialists such as Lakeland and Bettaware.

Finally, think about outside. If you are living aboard some lockable pods on the roof work well – just look on them as you would the boot of your car. If you have a permanent base, lockable cabinets or even self-storage units are well worth investigating, with most marinas offering facilities of some kind.

Also think laterally. Why have umpteen different electronic chargers when one multi-functional one may do the job of them all – and whilst on this subject a number of solar chargers are now coming onto the market which will do all this without even the need to drain your batteries! When it comes to entertainment why take up shelves with CDs when one iPod will store a whole library on a piece of kit so small it's easy to lose! Equally, vacuum bags can be used to pack winter bedding down by at least a third.

FURNISHINGS

Both soft and hard furnishing take on different qualities when placed in the context of a boat. Both need to be easily cleaned and compact.

Curtains will necessarily be small and constrained by bars to keep them from flapping about, but they offer a rare opportunity to add a dash of colour which will help define the tone of your interior, while at the same time offering a chance to demarcate different areas.

Chairs and other fixed or semi-fixed items of furniture need to be viewed through different eyes. Is there any possibility that they can be turned to more than one use? Can that stool also act as the rest for a fold-out bed, for example, and can that banquette also act as a storage area? The possibilities are endless – you just have to be minded to look for them.

LIGHT AND VENTILATION

Most boats come fitted with aluminium single-glazed windows as standard, although it is possible to go for higher specifications, including double glazing or anodised windows. The latter are worth considering as it is on the frame that most condensation will gather, and double glazing is also worth investigating, since windows are the most vulnerable point on a boat for thieves and vandals, to say nothing of the insulation benefits, although this does come at a fairly hefty premium for narrowboats and river cruisers.

An antique gimballed oil light.

A twin-flywheel Lister engine.

A Gardner engine.

A yet-to-be-ballasted new boat, primed, but not quite ready.

Portholes tend to be thicker and can feel more romantic, but they do have the downside of letting in less light. This can be a serious issue for the solitary liveaboard, at best inconvenient, and in severe cases even leading to cases of seasonal affective disorder. Alternatively, roof lights may seem like a good option, but they can be prone to leaking. If you really want to incorporate portholes in your home one idea is to design your boat to have a 'safe area' which uses portholes for its light and is capable of being secured. This can then be used to store your most valuable items when you are away.

Standard domestic double glazing units should be seen as entry-level for houseboats, which being static, can be more flexible about where they locate their windows. As the houseboat liveaboard knows what their view is going to be they can decide what it is they want to look out on and what it is they want to avoid!

By their very nature boats tend to be dark environments. For those lucky enough to have access to mains electricity, your lighting options are very similar to a domestic house. If you have either a 12V supply or a limited 240V supply then you need to opt for low-voltage lighting using diachloric bulbs, which have largely replaced the fluorescent alternative. Lighting can be a drain on your batteries, especially as you are most likely to be using them when the engine isn't running, and this will necessarily limit the number of lights you can have blazing away at any one time. It may be sensible in some areas to have push-lens battery lights.

A wide variety of styles of lights are available, ranging from reproduction Victorian brass through to ultra-modern spotlights in chrome and gold finishes. Once again, think about what your lifestyle is likely to be – will you be doing a lot of reading, for example, and do you want spotlights or something a little more intimate in the sleeping area? Ceiling lights tend to be recessed, for obvious reasons, and whilst wall-mounted lights may look nice they can also be a nuisance if they are on a main thoroughfare. Candles are not advisable, although oil lights remain quite popular for mood lighting, usually gimballed and wall-mounted. They can, however, be dirty and smelly and should really only be used for effect.

On a similar theme, ventilation is an easily missed consideration on a boat. Liveaboards are essentially living in an enclosed metal, wooden or fibreglass box through all seasons, and efficient ventilation is a must not only to keep a flow of air going but also to provide a means for unwanted gases to escape. Both high- and low-level ventilation are the subject of set marine standards which have to be followed when fitting out a boat. The most common form of basic ventilation is mushroom vents in the roof, either in traditional brass or stainless steel, although ventilation grilles will also be necessary near any gas appliances.

TO DIY OR NOT

Once you have decided your basic layout the question arises whether to do it yourself or get someone else to do it – or maybe a mix of the two. It is possible to buy basic hulls to work on and equally possible to buy an existing boat and convert it to meet your specification – although inevitably this latter option will require some deconstruction before you get into the reconstruction!

This decision may be driven by considerations of time, cost, will and, most important of all, competency. However tempting the option of doing it yourself may seem, if you are to live on board your boat you will be confronted with any errors on a daily basis. Charged with optimism, most potential liveaboards with a hankering to fit out their own boat tend to underestimate each of these considerations and the following is intended to offer some guidelines to help you make some realistic decisions.

A spacious
and light
feel is
possible.

A Rayburn
cooker on
board.

A good example of a well fitted-out kitchen. (Courtesy Kingsground Narrowboats)

A permanent double bed installation on a narrowboat. (Courtesy Kingsground Narrowboats)

An example of a light and spacious fit-out. (Courtesy Kingsground Narrowboats)

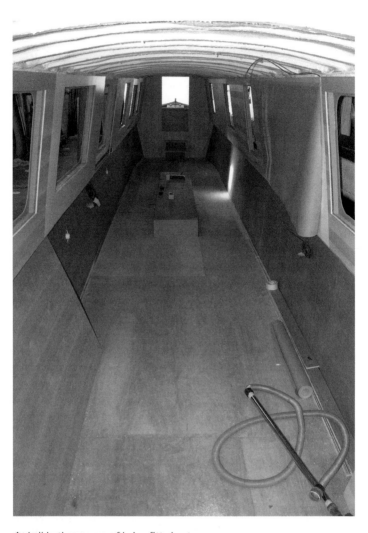

A shell in the process of being fitted out.

When calculating the time required to fit out a boat a rough rule of thumb for the novice is to allow two days per foot of boat, so a 60ft boat would require 120 days. That may not seem too bad but each of these days represents at least eight solid hours at the coalface and excludes any time spent in preparation, planning and shopping, in other words this assumes you have the materials you need delivered and on hand along with the tools and knowledge to convert them into the finished article. This extra time should not be underestimated.

When it comes to the necessary skills, remember that you will need to be a jack of all trades – carpenter, mechanic, electrician, decorator, gas installer, fitter and plumber. It is unlikely that you will posses all these skills, and some tasks will require a qualified professional, and getting someone in to do selected tasks will reduce the number of days you will need to spend on the task and it should be possible to arrange these to dovetail with your own time, thereby improving the efficiency of the process. It will, however, have an impact on cost.

When it comes to costs these will be driven largely by the level of specification you require and as with all large DIY projects it is prudent to allow a decent contingency on top of any final figure. Budgeting is important and needs to be kept on top of if you are not to end up with a nasty shock. A (very rough) rule of thumb for fitting out costs is anywhere between £150-250 a foot.

If you have the time, inclination, skills and finance to do it yourself there's little that can beat the sense of achievement of fitting out your new home yourself. As any regular viewer of Channel 4's *Grand Designs* will know, it is always more work than you thought it might be, and usually more expensive too! Equally, as the one example of fitting out a boat used on that show demonstrates, the downside of getting it wrong can be pretty deep!

Communications will almost certainly be wireless for at least part of the time.

Accessing power from a shore line.

Wind can provide a useful supplementary source of power.

Large solar panels can become a major source of energy if you are permanently moored.

Electrics, telecoms, water, drainage – all the various life support mechanisms you need, connected to the shore.

You can have a washing machine, but it may involve compromises.

QUESTIONS FOR LIFESTYLE AND LAYOUT:

- What is absolutely essential for you to maintain your lifestyle or the lifestyle you aspire to as a liveaboard?

- What do you want your boat to look like inside, and what feel are you trying to achieve?

- Are there any fundamental constraints on your layout? Is there anything that has to go in a certain place?

- How do you want to proportion the interior of the boat? Aim to be open plan to avoid claustrophobia.

- Make sure you allow enough space to have a permanent bed.

- Don't use holiday boats as a template – look around at what other liveaboards have done.

- Don't forget ventilation.

- Get the dual-use storage mindset.

- Consider all the elements involved carefully before doing the fitting out yourself.

- Consider the living area you want. Make sure it isn't simply the space left over after everything else.

Chapter 6
Electrics

Electricity is such a fundamental part of modern living that we tend to take it for granted. It is only when we have an unexpected power cut that we realise quite how dependent we are on it. What's more, our reliance on this precious and invisible commodity has increased in recent times, with government statistics showing a rise of 30 per cent per household in domestic use of electricity over the past thirty years.

Whilst there are a number of explanations for this, one important factor is the sheer number of electrical appliances we have and the power required to work them. Good examples of this are plasma TV screens, which tend to be both bigger and hungrier when it comes to electricity, consuming four times as much as a cathode ray tube TV; as well as our careless use of the standby button.

Above: *A built-in diesel-powered and water-cooled generator.*

Left: *A compact electrical installation showing inverter, 240 RCD trips, 12V fuses. The switch in the centre allows the user to select between 12V and 240V.*

Fitting Thinsulate to a new narrowboat. (Courtesy Kingsground Narrowboats)

A solid-fuel stove being used to keep a pan warm.

Pumping out – DIY style.

Heed the warning!

These are all luxuries the liveaboard cannot afford. Even if your mooring offers a 240V 'hook up' it can be a salutary experience to watch the numbers showing your consumption click round, and as soon as you slip your mooring you will be on your own, a self-sufficient unit operating under the very simple equation that you will only be able to consume what you can generate, store and transmit.

This chapter will therefore cover these three dimensions of electricity on board and go on to look at what might be considered the fourth leg of the table: consumption. It also includes a brief examination of an often overlooked side-effect of electricity when it comes to boating: the damage it can do to your craft and how you can protect it. Before all that however, it's worth pausing to consider some basics, with apologies to those for whom this is meat and drink.

BASICS

Electricity is a form of power, which is defined as the ability to do work. It is made up of electrons which are too small to see and will flow, if given the chance, around a circuit, and when it does this the flow is known as a current. Although water and electricity are notoriously bad mixers, water can be a useful analogy to use when considering the properties of electricity, which is useful given that water is a major preoccupation of this book! Circuits need to be closed to provide a current and if they are open then the flow automatically stops – in this way electricity is not like water, namely it does not simply flow out of a wire if there is a breach.

The 'strength' of an electrical current is measured in amps, although it is expressed in mathematical terms by the letter 'I'. We will see why this is important in a moment. The driving force behind that flow is known as the voltage or 'V' and the factors within the circuit which impede that flow are known as resistance or 'R', with appliances a good example of resistors, although as we will see there are others.

The relationship between these three components was neatly summed up 180 years ago by Georg Ohm, who devised the simple equation $V = I \times R$, from which it's possible to calculate exactly what's going on within an electrical circuit. Such was the significance of Ohm's discovery that his name is used to describe the SI unit of resistance. Following basic mathematical principles, $V = I \times R$ can also be expressed in other ways such as R=V/I or I=V/R. If you know two of the three basic components in your equation (and it is usually easy to get these from labels and packaging) you can use Ohm's Law to calculate the third – for example, if your load has a resistance of 4 ohms and the voltage source is 12V then your current will be 12/4 i.e. 3amps. Power, expressed as watts, is equally easy to understand using the equation P=VxI, and using these mathematical tools it is easy to grasp what is happening where within your electrical system.

Given your likely reliance on electricity as a liveaboard this basic understanding will be important to help you regulate your system and make sure it is in balance, as well as to diagnose the inevitable problems when they occur. Not for the liveaboard the luxury of simply assuming the electricity will just happen, you will need to keep a constant eye on the inputs and outputs involved and on maintaining that balance.

GENERATION

Most electricity on boats is generated as 12V direct current, although it can also be supplied as a 240V alternating current. It is known as alternating current because it is produced using magnets rotating between coils wound in opposite directions, which means that the current produced changes polarity as it is produced, causing the electricity to oscillate in a sine wave, with one complete wave known as a cycle, with the number of cycles a second known as frequency, measured in hertz.

If you have the benefit of mains electricity you will receive AC, whereas if you are generating your own electricity on board and storing it in batteries this will be DC. This is important as it will determine the sort of circuit you will have on board and how you power appliances – a 240V AC television will not work directly off 12V DC for example. As most liveaboards will want to have the convenience of using 'normal' domestic AC appliances, the solution is to have a means of converting self-generated 12V DC power into 240V AC, which is achieved using an inverter. 12V DC appliances are available, from kettles to TVs, with many produced to be run off car batteries, but they are rarely as satisfactory as the range of ordinary appliances available in every High Street shop, and they also tend to be expensive.

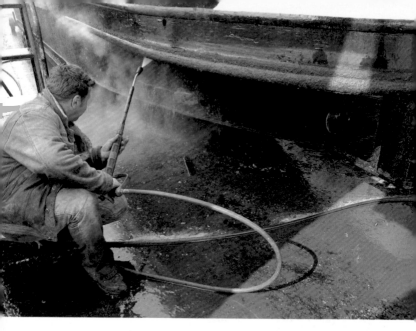

Using a power lance to get the hull clean before working on it. (Courtesy www.grannybuttons.com)

You cannot afford to neglect your paintwork.

Painting is a recurring job that shouldn't be neglected.

You can be as colourful as you like – it's your boat!

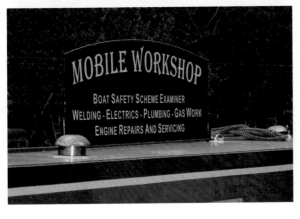

Calling out a mobile workshop can be the price you pay for neglecting general maintenance.

A 6KVA silent diesel generator.

A small 'suitcase' generator, quiet and useful, but needs to be stored.

Inverters convert 12V DC produced on board into 240V AC, with modern versions also charging your batteries and allowing for a convenient switch between landlines and batteries. They can also act as an energy management system along with dials and measures to monitor inputs and outputs, as well as ensuring that you are delivered perfect sine wave power, which is very important if you plan to use a computer on board.

This is where the equations mentioned above become important as when choosing your inverter you will need to have a good idea of what your likely power requirements are going to be – and then add at least 50 per cent if your budget will allow. In practice you will have five main options for sourcing electricity, with the opportunity to 'mix and match' along the way:

- A main electricity link

- Engine-driven alternator

- Generator

- Solar power

- Wind power

Mains is the most convenient source, but do not make the mistake of assuming that all you have to do is hook up and you can have as many appliances as you want. In practice, power will be limited and relatively expensive.

Solar power can help top up your batteries.

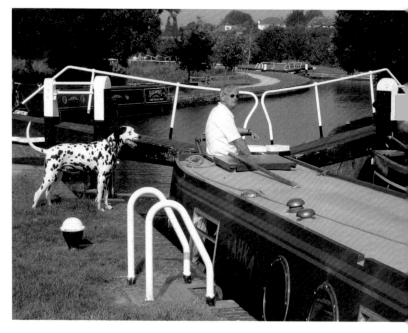

Dogs are great companions but need to be trained.

Wash day.

Ropes should be kept clean and tidy.

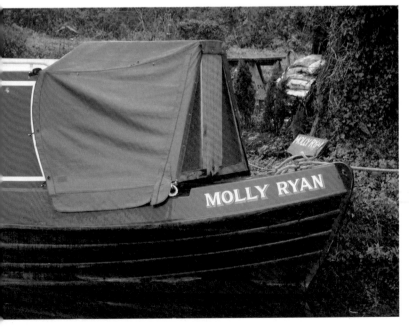

A cratch can provide cover to a potential thief.

An engine-driven alternator is the most common way of generating electricity when on the move. This has been covered to some extent in Chapter 4, but in short your diesel engine is powerful enough to generate DC electricity which can then be stored in your batteries (see below). This can in turn be passed through the inverter to produce 240V AC. Typically, boats have one battery dedicated to powering the starter motor – so that you won't be left stranded by watching too much TV – and then at least one more to power the domestic system. An alternator will be fitted to charge the former, and on more modern engines another, larger alternator is attached to charge the latter via an extra pulley on the crankshaft.

A bank of batteries.

Separate generators can also be used to produce electricity, using either petrol or diesel. These can be hooked up to provide power straight into your system, although care should be taken to ensure that all 240V circuits are protected by circuit breakers as, being surrounded by water, your system cannot be earthed in the way that a normal domestic system might be. This is not an area for cutting corners. Generators can be relatively compact, measuring as little as a small suitcase, and can be useful for topping up your power if you haven't been cruising and are not near a hook-up.

Generators do offer some disadvantages. Because of the fuel they use and the fumes these give out they have to be kept outside, as do your stocks of fuel, with all the associated security concerns – generators are designed to be portable and as such are tempting targets for thieves. It is possible, however, to buy water-cooled generators which fit into the engine compartment and draw their fuel direct from your main diesel tank. But whichever type you use, they can be noisy and should be used with consideration, especially when near other boaters or in a built-up area. The noise a generator makes can be deceptive, if you are inside watching TV or listening to your favourite rock band on your (electricity-powered) music system.

Solar power is becoming an increasingly popular option as the technology improves, offering both financial and environmental benefits. Receiving solar power does require an upfront investment, with costs if anything going up rather than down, as manufacturers are struggling to keep up with rocketing worldwide demand for their products. Solar panels are often quite large and are unlikely to reliably fulfil all your power requirements. That said, they can be a useful component of your power generation mix.

Solar panels typically use silicon cells and can come in a variety of forms. At one end of the spectrum they may be rigid and framed and may need permanent fixing, while at the other end they can come in flexible 'mats' which can be rolled out along your roof when required and taken in again afterwards. If you opt for permanent panels be aware that this will limit the use of your roof for other purposes, such as storage, flowerpots or sunbathing.

One increasingly popular option is to go for adhesive-backed panels which can be stuck to a roof to fit its curvature, and this is important as one of the determinants of the effectiveness of solar panels is the angle they present to the sun. Another important factor to consider is the most obvious, since although direct sunlight is not needed to generate electricity it does have a bearing on how much is produced. If you

A moveable houseboat.

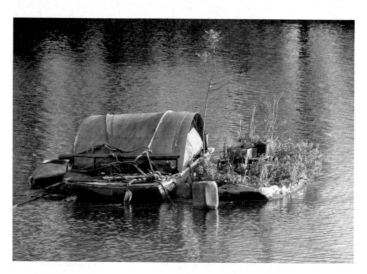

This garden actually floats, which means the owner never has to leave it behind!

Opposite top: *Narrowboats and houseboats living side-by-side.*

Opposite middle: *Having a boat doesn't mean you can't be a gardener.*

Opposite bottom: *TV aerial, garden, generator – looks like a liveaboard.*

spend a lot of time in the same location you may also wish to consider shadows, and more importantly shade from nearby trees, and how these vary across the day and year. Taking these into account can halve the stated power rating of a bank of solar panels – this rating indicates what the panel is capable of, not what it will necessarily deliver.

Once again, solar panels represent an exercise in achieving the best balance – here between surface area, power requirements and cost. In practical terms most panels used on boats can supply around 70W. What does this mean in real terms? Some simple calculations based on the demands of some key appliances can help, such as:

- 4 x 20W lights used for four hours = 320W

- 1 x 40W TV used for three hours = 120W

- 1 x 50W water pump used for half an hour = 25W

- TOTAL = 445W

A 70W solar panel receiving twelve hours of sunlight would in theory generate a total of 840W, but operating on half efficiency would provide only 420W – in other words, a useful contribution but not a total solution, given its unreliability and the fact that this calculation excludes a fridge, the most power-hungry of all appliances, seeing that it is typically on all the time!

Returning to the issue of cost, estimates vary but depending on use, and assuming you live on board all year round, solar panels can have a payback time of between 3-5 years, although this does not factor in the non-quantifiable benefit of generating your own carbon-free – and noise-free – energy. Panels can be fitted relatively easily but they must have a blocking diode fitted to prevent reverse current flow at night.

Wind power is also attractive from a green perspective and there are a range of small turbines available for the boat owner. Many of the calculations regarding solar power apply equally here, though turbines have their own pros and cons. They can be particularly effective if you tend to stay for long periods in non-sheltered spots (although this may carry other disadvantages), although they need to be erected and taken down each time they are used. The balance here is between size and power, the larger turbines generating more power, but needing more wind to get going in the first place. They can also be quite noisy, unlike solar panels. On the other hand, wind tends to be more plentiful in the non-summer months and a combination of solar and wind energy could provide a useful year-round supplement to your engine-produced power.

STORAGE

Since you will not be using your power as it's being generated, you need to store it until required. This is achieved using lead-acid batteries, which are essentially a mix of chemicals and metal used to preserve and discharge those little electrons. The secret to good electrical storage lies in battery maintenance, with digital voltmeters a must to monitor condition and capacity. Batteries are also expensive to replace and can represent a significant ongoing cost – they should not be taken for granted.

Batteries should be of the deep cycle or traction type and need to be kept in a well-ventilated compartment as they give off hydrogen gas, which is explosive. Fluid levels should be topped up regularly with distilled water, unless they are of the gel or the maintenance-free, sealed types. Battery terminals are of critical importance and should be covered to prevent anything metal, such as a dropped spanner, falling across them, which can cause an explosion.

They also need to be kept free of corrosion and grease, as this can cause a circuit to form and accelerate the speed at which the batteries discharge. But they will slowly discharge anyway if left alone, and this can be another benefit of solar panels which can be wired up to trickle-charge batteries if you have to leave them for periods of time. Smaller 20W units are useful for this purpose.

TRANSMISSION

Having generated and stored your electricity you need to get it to your appliances and make it work for you. This is where your knowledge of Ohm's Law comes to the fore, as moving electricity around means wires and wires constitute part of the 'R' in V=IxR. The longer the wire between an appliance and the batteries the more electricity will be used up getting it there, resulting in a drop in voltage. For this reason, it is better if heavy users of electricity, such as your fridge, are as close to the batteries as possible.

Furthermore, there are clear limits on the thickness of wire required to convey electricity. Too thin and they will get hot and become a potential fire hazard. Too thick, on the other hand, and there will be an unnecessary drop in voltage. Also, Ohm's Law tells us that the lower the voltage the higher the current, which means that a 12V system will require thicker wiring than 240V. All wiring also needs to be protected by the correct fuses. Most liveaboard boats tend to have 240V systems wired as a ring main, with conventional 13A sockets – which also need to be fused.

CONSUMPTION

The other side of the generation equation is consumption and there are a number of tricks to use to keep the equation in balance. The first, as hinted at earlier in this book, is to take a serious look at what you actually need, not just in terms of 'stuff', but also in what the 'stuff' consumes. Start by drawing up a list of the absolute necessities and then broaden this out to include 'love to haves' and then a greyer list of 'nice to haves'. Apply your knowledge of the basics of electricity to identify your power needs and start to do deals with yourself over where your priorities lie, and whether you prefer to simplify both your electrical needs and the chore of supporting them, or whether you would rather keep both the gadgets and the difficulty of powering them.

Absolute necessities are likely to include lighting and power for things like pumps. Then consider which form of energy you want to power other necessities such as cooking, heating and the fridge, all of which have gas alternatives. Electricity drawn off your sockets may be used to power gadgets, notably kitchen gadgets such as kettles and possibly toasters (but again, a gas cooker provides a good alternative for both) and entertainment such as music, TVs, DVDs and so on. Even within these components there are options, however, with digital music players, low-energy light bulbs and more efficient fridges. Electrical luxuries may include dishwashers, washing machines, irons and freezers, and although all these are possible, having them will involve a trade-off against other appliances or additional sources of power.

PROTECTION

Something a boat owner has to consider with regard to mains electricity, especially if they spend a lot of time in a marina or near other boats, is hull corrosion. What is known as a galvanic reaction takes place whereby one boat acts as an anode and an adjacent boat as a cathode, the pair effectively forming a battery with a chemical reaction taking place between them which results in any steel exposed to the water being attacked. This is not something to be taken lightly, with bad pitting sometimes visible on the hulls of two- or three-year-old boats, with some canals and rivers worse than others. The problem will be particularly noticeable where there are two different types of metal involved, with the metal more susceptible to corrosion taking the brunt. This may affect not just hulls but also other metal components in the water, such as propeller shafts.

Steel-hulled boats should, as a matter of course, be fitted with sacrificial anodes which will corrode before the hull and therefore require regular inspection and replacement as necessary. If they do not rot this could well be a sign that your hull is taking the bulk of the damage. One anode on the bow and one of either side of the stern, with additional anodes along the sides if necessary depending on the length of your boat and local conditions, would be typical, with different types required for salt and fresh water (it is worth checking you get fitted with the right type). Also, the anodes should not be painted over when the hull is blacked and they do need to be kept weed-free, so they are worth checking from time to time.

A pair of sacrificial anodes with the boat in dry dock, showing one almost totally eroded and another new one just fitted.

But anodes on their own may not be enough. Marinas offering mains power tend to do so via cables which are strung together around the earth cable in the shore power leads, and whilst essential for safety these also create an excellent conductor, making it easier for a current to build up and accelerating any potential damage (see Diagram 1). The solution to this problem is a galvanic isolator (see Diagram 2).

Diagram 1. (Courtesy Safeshore Marine)

Diagram 2. (Courtesy Safeshore Marine)

Above left: *A selection of hot water cylinders.*

Above right: *A 12V fluorescent light and smoke detector – the latter is an essential accessory.*

Above left: *A 240V wall light fitting and a 12V diachloric spot.*

Above right: *12V and 240V wiring at the installation stage. (Courtesy Kingsground Narrowboats)*

Right: *A diesel-fired domestic central heating and hot water boiler.*

In summary then, electricity is something the liveaboard cannot take for granted, with a happy harmony requiring thought and planning. This is true both in terms of balancing generation and consumption, and in creating the most appropriate 'mix' of power sources for your boat, position and lifestyle.

QUESTIONS FOR ELECTRICS:

- What range of appliances do you need to live successfully on board?

- What other appliances would you like?

- What potential is there in your list of appliances for energy-saving options?

- Calculate your power requirements, add some room for manoeuvre and work backwards from this.

- Will you be using mains power at any point during the year?

- Balance your power requirements with the different options open to you for generation – remember to include considerations such as convenience, environmental impact, noise and cost in your calculation.

- Have your electrical system checked for long-term reliability and safety. Electricity is one of the few areas with the potential for catastrophe and isn't worth gambling with.

- Make sure your boat is protected against potentially harmful corrosion from below the waterline.

Chapter 7
Heating, Cooking and Sanitation

The clearest divide between liveaboards and leisure boaters is probably the seasons. Whilst leisure boaters can dream of gliding gently along the waterways with the sun to their back, accompanied by baby ducklings and the sound of beer bottles opening, liveaboards know that in time the seasons will change and with it the cold and wet will return. It is essential therefore to make sure that your boat is more than a holiday caravan that just happens to be able to move under its own steam, but is capable of taking all that the Great British Climate can throw at it.

INSULATION

Very little separates the boater from the elements, and the first consideration should be the type and level of insulation your boat has. Good insulation should be able to keep you warm in the winter and cool in the summer. If you are in the happy position of choosing what form of insulation your boat has you will need to balance considerations of efficiency (measured in terms of its K-value: the lower the value, the more efficient it is); its bulk (you have limited space to play with so you don't want to use it up with something you won't see) and finally its cost. If you are fitting your own insulation you may also wish to consider how easy or difficult it may be to fit, and even if you aren't, this will have an impact upon the cost of fitting it – although it should be stressed that good insulation is one of those areas it isn't worth stinting on; it's very difficult to fix afterwards.

There are five main types of insulation material, the relative merits of which are summarised in the table below. A key factor in determining a good insulation material is whether or not it allows moisture to form behind it, as dampness here will slowly attack both wood and metal and rot the superstructure from the inside. The five types are:

SPRAY FOAM	Polyurethane foam applied in a spray which then expands. This material bonds to metal or wood and its closed-cell structure means it is impermeable to moisture. This is the most common insulation applied to newer narrowboats and until recently could only be applied by specialist contractors, although recent advances in technology are now enabling DIY kits to be produced.
FOAM BOARDS	These can be comprised of polystyrene, polyurethane or Polyisocyanurate foam pre-applied to boards for ease of fitting. The boards are cut to size and attached to battens, although the cutting can be a precision job if you are not to waste a lot. Boards are more DIY-friendly, needing less specialist equipment, but getting a tight fit is essential and they need to be vapour-sealed.
ROCK WOOL	Available in rolls or batts (a compressed version that looks a bit like a board). This is the sort of insulation seen in most house lofts. Rock Wool is easily applied, although it too has to be vapour-sealed. Cheaper than the alternatives, Rock Wool is only around half as efficient as foam and will therefore take up more of your precious space. Rock Wool can be applied by the amateur but needs to be handled with care because the fibres it is made up from require the use of masks and gloves.
THINSULATE	Available in rolls, this too can be fitted by the amateur by cutting it to size, gluing it into place and vapour sealing to avoid gaps. Thin but expensive, Thinsulate also has a relatively poor K-value, on a par with Rock Wool.
EXPANDED POLYSTYRENE	This tends to be found in older boats and must be fireproofed before use. Where this material is used, PVC wires have to be run through conduits as continuous contact rots the insulation. Expanded polystyrene was cheap, which explains its previous popularity.

RELATIVE MERITS OF DIFFERENT INSULATION MATERIALS

MATERIAL	BULK	COST	EFFICIENCY	EASE OF INSTALLATION
Spray Foam	Medium	Medium	Medium	Best done by a specialist
Foam Boards	Medium	Medium	Medium	Medium but time-consuming
Rock Wool	High	Low	Medium	Medium
Thinsulate	Low	High	High	Medium
Expanded Polystyrene	Low	Low	Low	Medium

Another consideration for potential heat loss is the windows, floors and doors. Double glazing is a serious option for liveaboards, offering the twin advantage of keeping heat in and noise out. It is not a cheap option, however, usually requiring sealed units to be made, with retrofitting often very difficult (although easier for portholes). Heat is also lost through doors and ventilation holes and although there is little that can be done about the latter, some basic insulation around the doors can reward the effort involved.

Use of Rock Wool as insulation.

HEATING

Assuming you have made your boat as snug as possible, a good heating system is essential, not only to keep yourself warm but also to stop the boat freezing up, and to keep it dry. In the height of summer it's often difficult to imagine how vulnerable your living space is to the cold, especially water pipes and anything else that contains water, such as pumps and water heaters. The boater has two main options on heating. The first is a central heating system and the second involves some kind of solid fuel stove. Central heating requires a boiler and this can be either gas- or diesel-fuelled, while solid fuel tends to be either wood or some form of coal, or a mix of the two.

There are few things more depressing than returning from a spell away to a cold damp boat with cold damp sheets and cold damp clothes hanging in the wardrobe. The speed with which your system can heat up your boat, combined with the need to keep Jack Frost at bay while you are away, can therefore be deciding factors when considering which option to go for. Central heating can be left on 'tick over', whilst solid fuel tends to be either on or off. Whether you expect to be away from your boat much in the winter – if it is cold, even just for a day at a time – is therefore a factor in deciding which way to go. It may also help to lag certain pipes, although if you suffer any damage it will inevitably be the one area you didn't protect!

Above left: *An attractive copper-clad diesel-fired heater.*

Above right: *A solid-fuel stove showing a heat distribution fan on the top. Beneath is not only additional storage, but a pair of slippers being warmed!*

It is worth remembering at this point that other features of a boat will also generate warmth, such as an inboard engine, the cooker, fridge and, not least, the people living on it, but these are unlikely to be enough on their own to keep you comfortable. The engine has to be running to generate heat, as does the fridge, although the colder months are likely to be the times when you are using these the least – indeed some liveaboards choose to turn their fridges off altogether in the winter to save electricity, it being just as sensible to keep food suspended from the pole outside.

Gas central heating typically involves an Alde-type boiler run off the gas bottle. These have the advantage of offering more-or-less instant heat and hot water, although they do accelerate your consumption of gas, so having easily accessible gas storage is a consideration, especially if you are going to be changing bottles in the cold. Alternatively, boilers can be diesel-fuelled, typically with a feed line from the main diesel tank, and some diesel-fired boilers are made to look like a traditional stove, giving them an added advantage.

Diesel boilers offer the same advantages as gas but do need regular servicing and de-coking, a job that can be messy, which is a particular consideration when you have to do it in what is effectively your front room. Also popular are diesel-fired heaters such as Eberspächer, Webasto and Mikuni, but these need regular servicing which tends to be very expensive.

Central heating does not come without its own problems. Systems need an electric circulation pump, and if the batteries run flat and this stops working, there is a risk that water may start to boil in the tank. They also need a header tank at the highest point and this isn't always something that is easy to achieve on a boat. Finally, systems need to be topped up with anti-freeze to avoid corrosion and to avoid the possibility of freezing pipes in the winter. Boilers can be plumbed into the hot water tank, which in turn may be kept warm using the engine cooling water via a calorifier.

Solid-fuel stoves come in various shapes and sizes and though they don't offer the same kind of instant heat, on the surface they may seem the simpler (and cheaper) option. But they can be difficult to regulate once blazing, and many a boater has fired up a solid-fuel stove only to find themselves sitting in their underwear or opening windows and doors to get back to a comfortable environment after an hour or so! Solid-fuel stoves can also be used to heat water through a back boiler.

The most efficient place to locate a solid-fuel stove is in the centre of the boat, although this is not always practical. One way round this is to install a heat-operated fan on top of the stove to circulate the heat. A number of efficient models are now on the market, although even the best model is unlikely to send heat to the extremes of a 60ft or 70ft boat.

When it comes to fuel, wood tends to burn faster than coal, but whatever you use needs to be stored somewhere, either on the roof or on the towpath if you have storage. Wood can generally be foraged for if you are on the move regularly, and as such offers a considerable cost advantage – once you have invested in the necessary chopping equipment and muscle power.

If using wood you should make sure that you clean the chimney often as tar builds up and blocks the flue. There are many brands of solid fuel; the most popular being Taybright, although Barge Nuts are also popular. Other types of fuel are Anthracite, Excel, Phurnacite and Homefire Ovals, although for the sake of the environment and out of respect for your neighbours you should always use smokeless fuel.

Stoves are also necessarily messy. Although most have ash cans for (relatively) convenient removal, if you are stationary you will need somewhere to deposit the ash. Another thing to bear in mind with solid fuel in particular is the need for adequate ventilation and a good carbon monoxide detector. Possible carbon monoxide poisoning is not restricted to solid-fuel stoves, as the gas is a by-product of the combustion of any carbon-based fuel including diesel and gas and all boaters should be alert to the possible signs and symptoms. These include so-called 'lazy' flames – ones that seem to be struggling to stay alight – and physical symptoms such as irritated eyes, headaches, nausea and dizziness – some of which can easily be mistaken for seasickness or alcohol intoxication. Carbon monoxide is sometimes known as the 'silent killer' and the gas can accumulate in areas such as the engine compartment. The threat it poses must always be taken seriously.

Whilst on the subject of safety, it probably goes without saying – but we'll say it anyway – that solid-fuel stoves do represent a very real fire hazard. Anything flammable should be kept well away from them, not something that's always easy in a confined space. The surrounding area, namely the back and sides of the fire, should be lined behind the tiles with Asbestolux or the equivalent, and there should be some form of hearth in the front of the fire to catch the glowing embers. They also need to be well secured and ventilated, with most having a detachable chimney on the outside of the boat, although it is all too easy to forget that the chimney inside will also get very hot!

But for the experienced liveaboard, a solid-fuel stove can be a friend, offering a visible source of comfort as well as a place to keep food warm (or even to cook it) as well as a place to dry gloves, socks and other small items. Given the various advantages and disadvantages offered by different heating options, it is perhaps unsurprising that many boaters go for a mixed system, combining the practicalities of central heating with the romanticism of a solid-fuel fire.

COOKING

When it comes to cooking, the most popular option is gas, although diesel cookers are becoming more popular. Electric cookers are also used, though only where it is possible to hook up to an external power supply. In most cases electric ovens and hobs will prove too power-hungry, and for the same reason, most boats will boil their water on a gas hob rather than use electric kettles.

The type of cooker fitted to a boat will depend on the type of boat it is. Wide-beamed boats such as Dutch barges may even have their own Aga-type stove, using either oil or solid fuel, whilst boats on a tidal mooring will tend to have gimballed stoves capable of swivelling to keep them level when the sea gets rough.

An Aga side-by-side with a gas stove.

Cooking is of course another potential hazard, and the galley area needs to be well designed and thought out, as well as being provisioned with safety features such as fire extinguishers and fire blankets. A final point worth noting may not seem obvious. Sink drain pipes should be as large a bore as possible and without a trap, as these tend to block up and smell. Remember all waste water runs into the river or canal so you should use environmentally friendly washing-up liquid and soap powder such as those made by Ecover.

SANITATION

Sanitation is perhaps the most basic function of all and one you will want to get right! It is also possibly the aspect of life that is most different on a boat. In a house when you flush your toilet you flush your troubles away, but on a boat this is only the beginning of the story, and your 'troubles' stay with you until you dispose of them.

There are a number of options when it comes to a boat toilet and you may find your choice limited by how you choose to live. A static boat, for example, will by definition find it difficult to access external pump-out facilities, although this does not necessarily rule out the pump-out option, as we shall see. A good idea can also be to fit solar-powered fan-assisted vents in your toilet/shower.

Unlike some European countries, canal and river craft in the UK are not allowed to discharge into the waters they ply – thank goodness – and so have to be equipped with some kind of holding tank. Traditionally this has meant either cassette or pump-out toilets, although more recently a third option, composting toilets, has come onto the scene. Toilet design owes a lot to the camping and caravan industry, with built-in toilets a relatively modern innovation. For the early boaters, a spade would have had to suffice!

Cassette toilets, or, as they are sometimes known, Elsan or porta-potti toilets, collect the waste in a cassette for disposal and involve the use of concentrated chemicals to keep odours at bay and allow multiple use before an opportunity arises for disposal. These chemicals, known as 'Blue' have a large amount of formaldehyde in them to kill off the anaerobic bacteria and also contain a large quantity of perfume, for obvious reasons. Formaldehyde is not a pleasant substance and should not come into contact with the skin. Alternatives do exist, including a substance known as 'Green', although these are of variable quality.

There are three basic types of cassette toilet. A simple plastic type with a self-contained water supply and a bowl and tank that clip together; a more sophisticated version with a plastic, floor-mounted toilet with an integral tank, which requires a trap door behind or at the side of the toilet to remove the cassette, and a third type which uses a vacuum, allowing the cassette to be fitted as far as 20ft away. These offer the added advantage of taking some of the odour away with them. With each the cassette has to be emptied at designated sites, and if you are left in absolute extremis that spade can come in handy again – although it is frowned upon.

Cassette systems are cheap and simple although they do have a limited storage capacity, which means you are advised to take opportunities for emptying whenever they come along. The issue of access can be a problem too and most boaters, certainly liveaboards, choose to keep a spare cassette, which can be a storage problem.

Pump-out toilets are very simple in concept. They work on a gravity discharge basis; that is, the waste falls straight into a holding tank, which then needs to be emptied using a vacuum hose, hence the term pump-out. Odour is again controlled using 'Blue', although not to the same levels. An alternative which some people find successful is to use live yeast. That said, smells can be a problem with both types of toilet, with the secret lying in frequent emptying and good disinfectant.

Pump-outs have the benefit of offering longer between emptying and the opportunity to give the tank a good old clean using fresh water. It should usually be possible to keep a holding tank clean, although some people just don't like the thought of sleeping with up to a month's worth of waste on board! Those with pump-out toilets have to be very careful about what goes down the pan, but having a 'proper' china pan is regarded as one of the benefits of a pump-out toilet.

Far left: *A toilet installation using a pump-out tank.*

Left: *A toilet using the cassette system.*

Above left: *An Elsan disposal point.*

Above right: *A bath made to fit a boat's space.*

The old adage that nothing should go into the tank that hasn't been eaten first is a good one, with even toilet paper sometimes being known to clog a pump-out system. Unclogging a pump-out is possible, but not particularly pleasant. Some pump-out toilets also have macerators or vacuums to allow the tank to stand a distance away from the pan, and these may also require less water for flushing. Macerators chop up solids and paper but will jam or break if ANY other object is put down the toilet. Their advantage is that the waste can be pumped through a small-bore pipe to a holding tank anywhere in the boat.

Pump-outs require a pump-out station, usually attached to marinas, although there are some self-service facilities, particularly on rivers. In the face of budgetary constraints, in 2007 British Waterways increased its prices for pump-outs, meaning a visit to have your tank cleared can cost in excess of £20 – a consideration if you want to empty it regularly. This has led to an increase in demand for 'self-pump-out' pieces of kit, which vary from hand-pumped versions through to electronic machines, both feeding a tank which then has to be emptied.

A well-fitted pump-out toilet will be fitted with a gauge so that you can tell when you are close to needing a pump-out. There is nothing worse than passing a pump-out facility and then finding out you needed it after all, with the next one two days away! A final consideration is to avoid placing the outlet to your pump-out on your roof if possible, as most pumps do not really have enough suction to cope with the extra height.

Compost toilets have recently come into vogue, although these are still very much in their infancy. These are water-free and require a constant supply of electricity to make them work. The waste needs to be aerated on a daily basis, with the electricity powering a small fan to keep odours at bay. Water evaporates away, although there is some evidence that current systems do not allow this to happen fast enough, resulting in unpleasant smells. If you are thinking of having a drinking party on board and have a compost toilet, some kind of secondary backup is probably a good idea! Furthermore, current designs tend to be bulky and not that attractive to look at. On the upside, a correctly functioning compost toilet will require emptying only once a year, representing a considerable saving, although you may pay in other ways! See 'Learn More and Links' for further sources of information on sanitation options.

Whilst on the subject of 'green' solutions, given their unique need to live as close to self-sufficiency as possible, liveaboards are potentially in an excellent position to take advantage of the new eco-friendly technologies now coming on stream. Opportunities may even exist to be pioneers of some of these new technologies, with solar power and recycling both good examples. Perhaps the area with the greatest potential is around water, a resource the permanent boater soon learns to value. Most current systems fitted to boats view water as a land-based householder might – as something disposable and of little value – while research into ways of reusing grey water generated on board a boat may pay dividends.

QUESTIONS FOR HEATING, COOKING AND SANITATION:

- How well insulated is your boat? If you are buying a second-hand boat check the material used and its K-value. If buying new make a balance between cost, bulk, efficiency and ease of application.

- How often do you expect to leave your boat in the winter? Do you need a trickle of heat and do you need to lag pipes?

- How long are you prepared to wait to heat up your boat and water? Do you need a boiler, and if so do you want it to be gas- or diesel-fuelled?

- If you opt for a gas boiler, how convenient are your spare bottles and how close are you to a gas stockist?

- If you opt for a diesel boiler, how happy are you about maintenance?

- If you opt for solid fuel, where will you keep stocks of wood and coal, and do you have somewhere you can dispose of ash?

- Ensure you have adequate safety precautions, especially carbon monoxide detectors, fire extinguishers and blankets.

- Is the galley near to the dining area?

- Is there good access to the sink and cooker?

- If going for a pump-out sanitation system, how convenient are facilities for pumping out, and have you factored the cost into your calculations?

- If going for a cassette-based sanitation system have you considered ease of access and storage room for a spare/used cassette?

Chapter 8
General Maintenance

As may have become apparent by now, living on board a boat requires a fair bit of dedication and knowledge, although, as with anything, this becomes less daunting the more it becomes part of your routine. It's all about adopting a fresh mindset. As part of this, there are a number of what might be called general maintenance tasks that you will need to keep on top of, some of which have been alluded to already.

The aim of this chapter, therefore, is to highlight the most critical of these, and to help you understand what to look out for and how to approach the issues that arise. As a liveaboard, many of the tasks set out in this chapter will become essential life skills, and even if you do not do them all yourself, you will need to know what it is that needs doing and to be able to check that they have been done correctly.

THE HULL

Your boat's hull is like the roof on your house, the main difference being that you can't put a bucket under it when it springs a leak. Your boat hull can be thought of as a tank, with any water or dampness accumulating in the lowest part of the bilges. Not only does water enter the hull from any leak, however small, below the waterline, but also from leaking hatch covers in the roof, leaking window frames (a very common problem), and any other container containing liquid on your boat, notably your water and pump-out tanks.

Leaks are always a problem, the trick being to trace them back to the source and tackle them there – rather than simply where they show themselves. Hatch covers can be especially tricky as you may be dealing with anything from a faulty seal to a design fault in the boat, whereas window leaks are easier to tackle. If the leak is only a small one, some silicon sealant will probably do the job. If it is more serious, caused by a build-up of rust between the cabin sides and the frame, then the frame itself will have to be removed, the rust treated and the frame primed and resealed with an all-weather sealant.

Leaking plumbing or a damaged tank are clearly more major tasks for which you may need expert help. Your responsibility is to be on the lookout for potential leaks, and to do this it is a good idea to have a piece of flooring that can be easily removed to access the bilges at the lowest point in the boat, which effectively acts as a sump. This should be inspected every month. Any build-up of water should be treated as a warning sign, and should be mopped or sucked out using a wet vac. At the same time it is a good idea to have some ventilation under the floor to prevent dry rot starting in the floor or bearers. If you have the luxury of building your boat from new, it may be worth considering protecting the bilges with a coat of Waxoyl before ballasting.

The subject of hull blacking has been touched on elsewhere in this book, and this should be seen as a regular act of maintenance which should be budgeted for. This applies to steel-hulled boats which need to be lifted completely out of the water (beware of so-called dry docks which do not run completely dry) so that their hulls can be cleaned off and repainted. Ideally this should involve cleaning all the weed and rust off the hull using a grit blaster, which is a specialist job and can be quite expensive.

The alternative to grit blasting is to use a power washer, and if you go down this route it should be done as soon as the boat is out of the water and the hull is still wet. Older craft may need regular professional inspections to satisfy your insurance company and if this is the case, this is the ideal opportunity to have a survey carried out by a marine surveyor.

When the hull has dried off all loose rust needs to be removed using a wire brush and the surface needs to be treated with an antirust preparation such as Rylard Rust Konverta. If you chose to use a bitumen-based paint (hull black) the manufacturer will recommend it should be applied to bare steel so do not prime with red oxide or zinc primer. Bitugard is made from coal tar and pitch, Comastic has vinyl added to the tar and pitch.

Hull black is a very thick paint so it needs to be applied using a large brush and rubber gloves. Eye protection must be worn at all times, and one-piece overalls and a hat are also recommended. More than one coat should be applied and you will need to follow the instructions on the tin, with some manufacturers recommending four coats on bare steel. The paint must be left to dry for at least twenty-four hours before returning the boat to the water. Two pack epoxy coatings are becoming more popular and, although initially more expensive, the paint will offer better protection and is more hard-wearing so it may be worthwhile. A further option that has recently become available is Zinga, which is a one-component anti-corrosion zinc coating that provides environmentally safe cathodic protection to steel and can be applied as though it were a paint. If you are using a third party for your hull blacking, an unannounced check to see that they are doing things correctly can be a good idea, as once the boat is back in the water you have no way of checking. Some boatyards will try to get away with a single coat, but this isn't enough.

Similarly, seagoing craft or those moored in tidal waters need to be coated with an anti-fouling paint once the weeds and barnacles have been removed. An anti-fouling paint suitable for freshwater inland waterways has also recently become available from Rylard.

Above left: *The equipment needed to shot-blast a boat – a professional task.*

Above right: *Shot-blasting in action.*

A selection from the range of available hull coatings.

Above: *The propeller and rudder of a narrowboat in the process of being cleaned. (Courtesy www.grannybuttons.com)*

Left: *A conventionally blacked hull, a Zinga-coated hull and a steel-primed hull.*

THE CABIN AND SUPERSTRUCTURE

The more visible part of your boat above the waterline also needs regular attention and the first step is to make sure you keep the paintwork in good condition by washing off the algae, moss, bird droppings and leaves, making sure that you clear drainage holes as you go along. Like car washing, this can be a relaxing Sunday afternoon activity, although you need to be careful when washing the non-towpath side of your boat, when a long-handled brush can come in handy if you don't feel like turning the boat around.

Car shampoo or Wash 'n' Wax-type preparations are fine, but ensure that whatever you use is friendly to the environment as it will be going straight into the water. Any sign of rust or chipped paint needs attending to sooner rather than later, as once rust gets under the paintwork it will spread very quickly – especially in a coastal environment. The rust will need grinding out, treating and priming before touching up with matching paint.

The superstructure of a narrowboat may need repainting once every four to five years, and this can be an expensive job so it's worth planning ahead and doing some research into preferred paints and colours. Some colours are more durable than others, with red particularly vulnerable to fading. For all but the very skilled, painting is a professional job and once again it is worth overseeing the work to make sure it is done correctly. In particular, you should check that the correct number of coats is applied – a call to the paint manufacturer will reveal the recommended coverage. Similarly, good sign writing can define the quality of a new paint job, so ask to see examples of the signwriter's work beforehand as these will usually be specialists drafted in specifically for the task.

WATER TANKS

Fresh water tanks can be made of polypropylene, stainless steel or mild steel and are integral to the hull. A tank can hold 150 gallons of fresh water and, as these tanks are usually located below the waterline, a pressurising pump is needed to make it flow to the domestic system. If the tank is made from stainless steel, polypropylene or galvanised steel it should be maintenance-free, provided that once a year sterilising tablets are dissolved in a full tank of water, as per the instructions on the packet.

Should the tank be integral to the hull under the forward cockpit deck, as is popular on narrowboats, it will be fitted with an inspection hatch. This needs removing once every two or three years to inspect, clean and paint inside the tank as the interior will become full of plant life and rust and quite put you off making a cup of tea from it.

There is only one way to clean this out – get inside and scrub! This isn't a pleasant or easy job but it is very important and should not be neglected. A 'wet vac' vacuum cleaner is indispensable, both for this job and for cleaning out the bilges. Having cleaned the tank out, let it dry, and then give it at least two coats of bitumen paint. Some hull blacks are suitable for this, but you should check the manufacturer's recommendations on the tin first. The inspection hatch needs to be replaced with a new gasket or silicon sealer, and it is a good idea to use stainless steel or brass bolts to secure the hatch cover so they can be easily removed next time.

ENGINE SERVICING

It is worthwhile getting to know your engine and what, quite literally, makes it tick. Regular maintenance will not only give you peace of mind but also reduce the chances of an emergency call-out, which can be an expensive and time-consuming business. Any diesel engine needs regular oil changes as set out in the operating manual. Deciding when to change the oil and filter will depend on how many hours the engine has been run since the last service, and you may wish to consider installing an hour counter within the rev counter or a separate gauge. Before the old oil is drained out, run the engine until it is at its working temperature.

Use the sump pump – if fitted – to pump the old oil out, otherwise the sump drain plug will have to be removed. If there is not room under the engine for a waste oil container, drop it into the bilges under the engine, then suck it out later with a wet vac. After this, remove the old oil filter and fit a new one, fitting new sealing 'O' rings if the filter is not of the spin-off type. Rubber gloves should always be worn when handling old engine oil as it is carcinogenic. Check the service manual for the correct grade and type of oil with which to refill the sump, as using the wrong oil can invalidate the engine manufacturer's warranty.

The fuel system on a boat is all-important – nine times out of ten any problem encountered with a diesel engine will be due to problems with the fuel system. Owing to the fact that the fuel tank is in a damp environment and subject to internal condensation, it is always best to keep the tank as full as possible – especially during the winter months. Many of the problems encountered with the fuel system are caused by water contamination in the fuel.

At the bottom of the fuel filter there is usually a drain plug. To meet BSS regulations this must be metal and not plastic, so that it can't melt if there is a fire and let the fuel pour out. Undo the screw periodically and drain into a transparent container (ideally glass) until all the water is removed and pure and clean diesel is coming out. The fuel, being lighter, will float on top of any water. Replace the drain plug. Having done this you shouldn't have to bleed the system. Should the engine still fail or misfire, the next thing to replace is the fuel filter.

A boat in dry dock having work done to it.

Fuel filters come in two main types: the older CAV replaceable element or the later screw-on type. Be aware that there may be more than one filter in the fuel line. Start by turning the fuel off at the tank – something you should check how to do from the manufacturer's instructions, as it is inevitable that at some point you will need to know how to do it – and then follow the instructions supplied with the filter. After fitting, turn the fuel tap back on and finish by bleeding the system – again, each engine is different and you will need to refer to the manual.

Good ropes are particularly important on tidal moorings.

OTHER REGULAR TASKS

Alternator and water pump drive belts need to be checked for cracks or wear and adjusted at least once a year (possibly as part of a pre-winter routine), and replaced as necessary. Another important part of any pre-winter routine will be checking your engine's cooling system, notably making sure it is protected with a strong enough antifreeze solution. This can be checked using a hydrometer, an accessory available from most car part shops, and you should be looking for a minimum of 40 per cent antifreeze. Having added antifreeze, the engine should be run up to operating temperature to make sure that it has mixed properly and circulated around the calorifier tanks. This also provides an opportunity to check for any hose leaks. The antifreeze should be left in year-round as it also acts as a rust inhibitor.

As raw water-cooled engines do not use antifreeze it is advisable here to drain the system before the first frost. Remember that fresh water will freeze more quickly than sea water, so if you are based on a river or canal you will need to be quicker on your toes.

While in the engine compartment it is also worth checking the stern gear. Grease needs to be sent down to the stern gear every other day when cruising, using the tap provided, and from time to time the grease supply will need replenishing. Should the stern tube gland start leaking, the solution is not, as is often thought, to send more grease down, but to either adjust the lock nuts which will need tightening, or to repack the gland. Automatic bilge pumps will also need to be checked to ensure they are operational and are clean. Failure to do so can be costly, as pumping oil out into the water is not only antisocial but can also result in a heavy fine.

Other pre-winter checks will involve the domestic heating system. Any central heating system will also need filling with antifreeze/rust inhibitor, with a 50 per cent mix advisable here. It is also a good idea to have an annual boiler service using a qualified engineer. Note that 'qualified' here does not just mean a CORGI engineer, but one with the necessary certification relating to LPG work on boats and caravans.

If you have a diesel stove, just before winter is also a good time to carry out the unpleasant task of having it de-coked and serviced. If you use a real fire then you will also need to clean out the chimney. This is a job best tackled from the top down using a brush and rod. Remove the baffle plate first and let the soot fall into the fire where it is more easily removed – a dirty but necessary job.

It can be all too easy to forget the state of your mooring ropes, which should be checked regularly for rot or fraying. Ropes used to moor a boat on a tidal river will necessarily receive more wear than those used on a boat in a non-tidal river or canal, and all ropes are more susceptible to rot in the winter. A snapped rope is every boater's nightmare, especially if it happens at night, and preventing it is perhaps one of the easiest of all the regular maintenance tasks.

Finally, when checking your ropes, it's worth giving your staging the once-over if you are on a permanent or semi-permanent mooring. Once again, rot and algae are the enemies here and you don't want the staging to give away, as if it does it will inevitably happen when you have your arms full of something precious, besides which a broken leg isn't much fun on a boat!

QUESTIONS AND NOTES FOR GENERAL MAINTENANCE:

- Check the bilges regularly and regard any build up of water as a warning sign.

- Fix leaks as soon as you spot them, making sure you tackle the source not just the symptom.

- Hull blacking and superstructure painting can be planned for and does not come cheap – make sure you get a quality job.

- A clean water tank is essential for your health – check it regularly.

- Engine servicing, notably oil and fuel filters and the fuel system, is something you can learn to do yourself, but check you have done them correctly.

- Consider drawing up a pre-winter checklist of maintenance tasks, including the engine cooling system and the domestic heating systems.

- Are your bilge pumps efficient?

- Good ropes give peace of mind.

- Is your staging sound?

Chapter 9
Finance

Having got this far into this book, and assuming your appetite to live aboard has been whetted, you've probably been on a journey that has oscillated between desire and trepidation but is now nearing its end with one great question still hanging in the air: how much is all this going to cost me? The answer, as is so often the case when it comes to money, is: it depends.

That said, this chapter will set out some rough rules of thumb and an indication of what you might be letting yourself in for. Before getting down to brass tacks, it is worth emphasising the truism that with boating, as with so many other things, you get what you pay for. When budgeting to live aboard, there are plenty of opportunities to prioritise expenditure according to your own personal preferences and chosen lifestyle.

Specialist agents can be found for different types of boat.

As a general rule, it's probably fair to say that living on board your own boat is much less expensive than living on shore, but don't make the mistake of thinking that the costs are insignificant – they're not. Those who ignore some of the basic maintenance costs outlined here will find that their 'economies' are nothing of the kind and will come back to bite you very quickly, and that they have the capacity to bite quite hard! The good news is that living aboard is not as expensive as that other waterborne activity, sailing, which one wit once described as the equivalent to standing in the shower and ripping up fifty pound notes – and that's only a hobby!

Given the wide range of variables and bearing in mind that the inland waterways remain the choice of the vast majority of liveaboards, the numbers discussed below are based upon a mid-sized (55ft) narrowboat, although they should provide a good template for others as well.

FIXED COSTS

There are certain costs you simply won't be able to avoid, but some latitude remains on how high you let them climb. No allowance has been made for depreciation, although if you follow the guidelines set out below, you should find that your boat holds its value fairly well. Your absolute fixed costs will be your licence and insurance, although as will become apparent, this isn't the end of the story.

Licence

Licence fees will vary according to where you want to cruise. If you intend to take full advantage of the inland waterways system, taking in both the rivers controlled by the Environment Agency and the canals operated by British Waterways, you will need a Gold Licence. Prices seem to be escalating above inflation and in 2009 (the licence is valid for a calendar year) a Gold Licence cost £888 if paid in full (add 10 per cent if paying by direct debit) for a 55ft boat. An annual Canals and Rivers Licence from British Waterways only would have cost £725 assuming payment up front. Assuming further above-inflation increases, allow £800 per year.

It is possible to reduce this, as, for example, there is a 10 per cent discount if your boat is deemed 'historical' and a 25 per cent discount if your boat is powered only by electricity, and there is also the option of a rivers-only licence, although this does restrict your freedom of movement considerably. If you have a houseboat with no means of propulsion at all, you need to apply for a Houseboat Certificate, although this costs the same as a Canals and Rivers Licence. Licences can be bought for three, six and twelve months, and options also exist to buy a shorter-term licence if you intend to moor up off the system over the winter. Up-to-date rates can be found on the boating section of British Waterways' website – www.waterscape.com.

Insurance

It is a requirement of your licence that you hold, as a minimum, £1 million of third-party insurance. The key words here are 'as a minimum' as it is likely, especially as your boat will also be your home, that you will want to go for a comprehensive policy, especially given the marginal cost difference and the fact that your boat will very possibly be your biggest asset. The waterways press includes a number of advertisements from marine brokers and the market is fairly competitive. All in all, for our sample boat expect to pay around £350 a year in total for insurance (including contents).

Council Tax

If you decide to live on a permanent houseboat, another fixed cost will be council tax, which will of course vary enormously according to where you choose to live but a (very) rough rule of thumb suggests you shouldn't expect to pay less than £1,000 per annum. If you are renting your houseboat and your finances are constrained, you may be entitled to apply for housing benefit which can help with the costs of the rent for the boat, mooring fees and the licence. Continuous cruisers and most other boats with at least the ability to move should find that they can avoid council tax although again, local authorities vary in their interpretation of the rules.

Maintenance

Although there is only one absolute fixed cost under this heading – the requirement to renew your Boat Safety Certificate – this brings with it other costs too. The cost of the survey required to gain the Certificate is fairly modest, especially when factored in over four years

– you should allow around £160 for the survey and the inevitable niggles that will need to be resolved, probably because the regulations have changed since you last had it done – but the process itself acts as a good discipline to get other sizeable but necessary jobs done at the same time.

The most obvious of these is getting the hull blacked. Views vary on how frequently you should have your hull blacked but the four-yearly cycle of the BSS operates as a powerful incentive to get your boat lifted completely out of the water (the cost of this has been included in the amount quoted above) and have a decent look around. Fresh anodes will also be necessary at this point. All told, a reasonable sum to set aside for this would be £500, although it is probably fair to say that four years is the absolute maximum you should leave blacking and every two years is better for budgeting – so, that's £250 a year, which makes an annual allowance of £300 when BSS and associated work is added.

Likewise, it's difficult to determine a precise interval for repainting, as your need will depend upon how many minor scrapes you have, the basic condition of your superstructure, the quality of the previous paint job, how decorative and intricate you want to be and whether you've gone off your existing colour scheme. Painting is also something that many liveaboards like to get involved with themselves, viewing touching up paintwork as an ongoing and not altogether unpleasant task.

But nothing quite beats taking your superstructure right back to bare metal and applying even coats of the various primers and undercoats required to provide the 100 per cent protection from the elements that you will need. Painting is an extremely time-consuming process and is an area where it is easy to fall for false economies. DIY painters are often easily spotted, as their boats never quite look like they're finished. Doing it yourself does save on labour costs, but boat paint is intrinsically expensive which is why painting has been included as a fixed cost.

Let's say you decide to have a 'back to basics' job done once every five years and keep on top of things yourself in the meantime. A professional stem-to-stern job, stripping back to metal and applying the various coats will cost in the region of £25 a foot, so that's £3,300 for our 55ft boat, or £660 a year. On top of this you need to add materials for regular maintenance and you will be looking at a minimum of £725 a year – a significant cost that is often forgotten.

Finally, assuming you are not a master mechanic, an annual service is probably a good idea. Again, this is not an absolute necessity but gambling on nothing going wrong is a high-risk strategy – you really don't want to get stranded in the middle of nowhere and have to find someone who'll come out to see you: a call-out charge will soon make you rue not having that regular check-up. At a minimum, your filters and belts should be checked and probably replaced, and it's a good idea to have the electrics and gas looked over as a matter of course. Once again, therefore, this has been included as a fixed cost and a fairly reasonable one at that – say £100. Add a little more if you want to buy the extra peace of mind of knowing you will be able to call out a professional, something you can secure by joining one of the various canal and river rescue companies which act as a sorting of boater's AA – details are available in the waterways press.

VARIABLE COSTS

Variable costs cover those items where you might think you have greater latitude, and whilst this is true to some extent, it is surprising how quickly those bills accumulate no matter how hard you might try to keep them down. The main variable costs are moorings and consumables, although once again, there are many others.

Moorings

The subject of moorings has been given its own chapter in this book and this serves to demonstrate the range of options – and costs – involved. The absolute minimum you can pay is nothing, assuming you either adhere to the continuous cruising rules, even in winter, or have some kind of arrangement with a kindly landowner. Both of these are likely to be the exception. The next step up is probably the boater who cruises for most of the year but moors up on a British Waterways site for, say, four months a year, which may cost as little as £500.

More likely scenarios involve a part-time base, although again, costs will vary according to whether this ison the towpath or in a marina, and those with a long-term base. As with most things in life you will get what you pay for, a marina mooring for example will include some services and it depends on where in the country you want to be as mooring prices tend to echo house prices in this regard.

For this reason, no single figure has been given for moorings as it could only represent an average and would therefore either be misleading or meaningless. If you want to go towards the bottom end of the scale, budget at around £500 per year, and if you want to head towards the more comprehensive end, allow around £3,000 per year. These figures are for the canals, and rivers will be significantly more. Also, if your home is a houseboat you probably want to move out of a mooring mindset and think more in terms of rent.

Consumables

Basic consumables will include gas and electricity (whether metered or generated yourself), fuel, and pump-outs. Gas will be bottled and you will need to keep a spare bottle at all times. Assuming you don't use gas for heating, a budget of around £125 per year might cover your needs, though double this if you do use it for heating – the difference being a reasonable budget for coal and wood (although it is possible for forage for the latter). Metered electricity has the advantage of allowing you to monitor use and security of supply, but this comes at a cost – in the region of £100 assuming you are only using it in the winter and are cruising the rest of the year.

Fuel will depend upon how much you cruise and run your engine, and this is where the hidden cost of generating your own electricity resides. Imminent increases in the cost of red diesel will impact here and a budget of around £300 is a reasonable target, although you may be able to come in slightly below this (although any saving will be marginal set against your total budget).

Pump-outs are a necessary cost, assuming you have this kind of arrangement, and is a cost that can accumulate. It can cost as much as £200 per year, assuming you don't have your own kit, but even then there is likely to be a disposal charge and you may wish to consider whether the effort required to make the saving is worth it.

Other costs are mostly discretionary, although it is advisable to factor in the cost of some running repairs and maintenance, as well as a sum to treat yourself to a fresh piece of kit, or to replace consumables such as batteries – which only last three to four years – into your annual budget. Say £500 for that. Items falling into the discretionary area have cropped up during the course of this book and include things such as onshore storage, a car parking space, a post office box and costs associated with mobile communications. Few liveaboards will be able to avoid all of these, and as such a sum of

£500 has been included here to be spent as you choose, which may be a little on the conservative side.

SUMMARY

ROUGH ANNUAL LIVEABOARD BUDGET	
Licence	£800
Insurance	£350
BSS and annual maintenance	£300
Painting	£725
Annual service	£100
Cooking and heating	£125
Diesel	£300
Pump-outs	£200
Other repairs, maintenance and equipment	£500
Sundry other costs	£400
TOTAL	£3,800

Taking all these costs together suggests a sum in the region of £3,800 a year, although this excludes moorings, any metered electricity and any council tax. As already highlighted, this should be taken as a very rough guideline and although there is some room for manoeuvre, it's not much, and there is a recurring danger that any economies may turn out to be false.

Houseboat hunting.

BOAT PURCHASE

Before you get involved with annual running costs you will, of course, have to buy your boat in the first place – assuming that owning your own boat is your goal, as is the case with the vast majority of liveaboards. While many boat purchases do not require financing as they are funded from proceeds elsewhere (the sale of a house, a legacy, a retirement or redundancy package), many others do, and it is worth pausing to consider some of the rules of this particular game.

Few conventional financial institutions regard buying a boat in the same way as buying a house. In recent times even housing has lost its allure as an asset against which banks and building societies are willing to loan money, so their attitude towards giving credit for a boat can be imagined. These institutions are likely to require something more tangible before they lend on a boat, and if you intend to retain a pied-à-terre for the winter months, one option may to be raise a mortgage on this. Otherwise, banks and building societies will probably only lend you the money on an unsecured basis, with all the implications this brings for interest rates.

Luckily, marine finance specialists exist (again, check the waterways press, but Barclays, the Bank of Scotland and Lombard are all key players in this area) who understand the idiosyncrasies of the boating world, but even these institutions are unlikely to offer you 100 per cent loans. If you are very lucky you may be able to borrow the total sum up to around £15-20,000, but after that the maximum you can probably hope for is 80 per cent.

Some loans are regarded as marine mortgages – that is, although the rate charged is lower than with a normal loan, the sum is secured against the boat – whilst others may be unsecured. As with houses, a survey and independent valuation will also be required. If the craft you intend to live on is one capable of traversing the high seas, you will find your creditworthiness sinking faster than an anchor as lenders have a (perhaps understandable) fear that you may never be seen again!

But this is only a brief introduction, as if you look like a reasonable risk, you will be offered a plethora of products – secured and unsecured, fixed and variable rates, mortgages and loans and even personalised packages. As such, independent advice may be a good idea, and there are plenty of brokers available to help you negotiate a way through the maze (see the waterways press), and going down the broker route may even end up saving you money in the long run.

QUESTIONS FOR FINANCE:

- Have you got the right type of licence?

- Have you checked whether you will need to pay council tax?

- Have you included a budget for recurring maintenance?

- How much of your own painting do you intend to do?

- Review your mooring options, considering that they may represent as much as half your annual running costs.

- Will you be paying for metered electricity?

- If you are buying a boat, use a marine finance specialist and consider using a broker.

Chapter 10
Survival Tips

So far this book has set out a host of advice to those considering the liveaboard life, but there is nothing that quite beats the smack of experience, so in this final chapter the authors are taking the opportunity to share some of their own survival experience, in the hope that elements of it may distil into wisdom.

This is not intended to be a comprehensive list, more a random collection of tips, and much of what is covered here may seem obvious. But we have taken the view that that is no reason not to state it, since after all, one man's obvious may be another man's revelation and the obvious has a disconcerting habit of being forgotten! We have clustered these tips under three headings: Safety, Security and Sharing.

SAFETY

The most basic of all safety survival tips is to have a good first aid kit. This is not the same as buying an off-the-shelf pack from your local chemist, but means thinking about likely contingencies and stocking accordingly. Most standard first-aid kits are long on bandages and short on medicines and you need to supplement them with a range of the sorts of day-to-day remedies you may need to dip into and may find difficult to get hold of when you are miles away from a doctor, dentist or pharmacy. Examples may include:

- Antiseptic creams, including nettle and sting creams.

- Painkillers such as paracetamol or Nurofen.

- Cold remedies.

- Something to tackle food poisoning.

- Antihistamines.

- Deep pain spray.

- Antacids.

It may also be a good idea to top up your first-aid knowledge by going on a course run by a recognised organisation such as St John's Ambulance before embarking upon the liveaboard life, and to stock up on things like insect repellent and disinfectant. Finally on the subject of health, if you are on regular medication it is probably as well to have a spare supply with you.

Other aspects of basic safety should not be taken for granted, including making sure that lifebelts and jackets are in good working order and are to hand. The same applies to fire extinguishers. Also, while on the subject of the basics, it pays to never keep your eye off your stocks of essentials such as food, fuel and water – easily forgotten but missed when they are not there. With water it is also worth considering the state of your water tank – do you need a filter for drinking water?

Other chapters have mentioned basic equipment you need to keep to hand, but experience also suggests you may wish to consider an alternative to one of your most elemental items of kit – matches, which have a tendency to get damp as soon as you turn your back. Alternatives include cigarette lighters or hand-held sparkers. Domestic batteries can also start to corrode when you least expect it, so a spare dynamo or solar-powered torch can also be a godsend.

Other items the liveaboard should always have spares of include fuel filters, drive belts (a full set) and a tube of silicone, along with some plastic padding to effect a temporary repair should you spring a leak. Think also about keeping a strong magnet on the end of a rope for recovering keys (and even windlass handles) that fall into the water. And just in case your cosy home becomes a tempting option as the nights draw in, a mouse trap or two may come in handy.

Experience also suggests that it's a good idea to know where you are in non-canal terms. So as well as having a canal guide, it's always worth having a road map on board should you need to jump ship and re-engage with the wider world. Being surrounded by water, you may also wish to have a 'Plan B' should your mobile phone end up in the drink. Record all your most important phone numbers in a book which you keep in a safe, dry place, since if you do lose your phone you don't want to lose all your numbers too. Alternatively, invest in a SIM card backup device. On the subject of phone numbers, it's a good idea to keep all relevant British Waterways and Environment Agency numbers handy in case of a sudden emergency – a laminated card being one option.

Considering where you moor is also another key determinant of your personal safety. Remember that conditions do change from season to season, and what might have seemed a perfect spot in the summer can be hopeless in the winter, especially if you get cut off by ice or snow – canals can freeze over! Equally, river levels can change and climate change seems to be bringing with it more extreme weather patterns, as witnessed by the bad floods of 2007 which occurred in the early summer – very much out of season. Finally, in the case of utter disaster do bear in mind the vital importance of having more than one means of escape from your boat!

SECURITY

Protecting yourself from the more unsavoury elements of society is as much a fact of life on board a boat as it is living in a house. If anything, boats should be regarded as more vulnerable – not only because they are harder to protect, but also because as strangers to an area, cruising liveaboards may be less aware of the dangers particular areas may bring.

Boats do get broken into, although instances of this are perhaps more unusual than popular myth may have you believe. Most break-ins are opportunistic, and there is much you can do to reduce the opportunities your boat offers to thieves in the first place. Much of this is common sense, such as not advertising that you have something worth stealing by leaving items of value on display near a window, or making sure you leave curtains closed when leaving your boat. Also consider what might be thought of as an item of value – this isn't necessarily just consumer goods, which may be of interest to a petty thief, but also food and alcohol which may attract itinerants or teenagers.

Above left: *A security bar offers extra protection when you leave your boat.*

Above right: *Lifejackets must be accessible.*

The idea of a 'safe area' which can be given reinforced security within your boat has already been suggested in an earlier chapter. Another good idea can be to bolt a safe to the floor under your bed for really important documents and other valuables. Finally, don't forget the items you routinely leave outside the cabin, which may include poles (handy for smashing windows), flowerpots (likewise), windlasses, lifebelts and decorative items. Some boats also have removable seating which offers another useful implement to the opportunistic thief.

Attention paid to making access to your boat more difficult is rarely wasted. Most thieves like to get in and out quickly and will thank you for having a cratch cover over your front cabin doors, as this provides them with cover while they work on your elaborate security measures. On the other hand, they will not thank you for forcing them to squeeze through narrow windows, so this is an area where portholes offer a benefit, and the sight of someone climbing into a boat via the roof usually arouses suspicions – so long as they can be seen. Boaters tend to operate a very effective informal neighbourhood watch system, and will look out for one another's boats.

Good locks and solid doors should go without saying, but there are considerations here. Hinges should ideally be on the inside so they cannot be unscrewed, and steel doors secured with an effective mortice lock are preferable to wooden doors secured with a padlock (which acts as a signal that you are out). Window frames should be riveted and not easily unscrewed, and you may wish to consider fitting security grills.

As well as thieves, boaters need to protect themselves against what politicians have come to call 'anti-social behaviour' – what most of us may regard as yobs and vandals. The actions of this crowd are rarely logical and can be extremely irritating, especially when cruising, and all the more so if you are transparently by yourself. Never underestimate the capacity of the individual with nothing better to do or too much drink inside them to simply throw your things into the water 'for a laugh', although quite who laughs at this is open to question.

As it happens, instances of stone-throwing, rope-cutting and 'steaming' (i.e. groups jumping onto one end of your boat and running through, picking up what they can and jumping off the other end before you know what's hit you) are actually pretty rare. Your best defence is probably to be on your guard in unsavoury areas and to have a digital camera on hand (although not somewhere where it can be snatched!). It's an item of kit that can act as a curiously powerful deterrent, if a potential miscreant thinks they are going to be identified after the event.

Finally on the subject of security, all instances of theft and vandalism should be reported to the authorities. Whilst the chances of a successful prosecution in individual cases are slim, an accumulation of reports can spur the police into action and help prevent future incidents.

SHARING

There is a tendency to look at the liveaboard life as a solitary activity, and whilst this is often the case, it isn't necessarily so. By definition, narrowboats are the least amenable craft for sharing, although plenty do share with a partner and sometimes even with children. But it is more usual with larger boats, in particular houseboats. Of course, having children on board opens up a fresh set of considerations, including the range of equipment required, different tastes in entertainment, and especially water safety. Then there's access to friends, health services and school to consider. All these issues are solvable, but involve an extra layer of considerations.

Pets can be easier to live with, especially if they live in a cage! Birds, hamsters and even rabbits and guinea pigs have all been known to provide company to liveaboards. Portable hutches and foldable runs are available, with the runs making it possible for your companion to feel the grass beneath their paws when moored at a grassy towpath.

Dogs are of course a boaters' favourite and although preferences over breed vary, expedience means that the smaller varieties are more popular. Unless your chosen breed is a natural swimmer, the ideal situation is to start them young, with dogs taught to swim as a puppy using a harness or buoyancy aids. Dogs also have a tendency to roam, and a collar tag saying where they live with a mobile number on it are a must.

Cats' aversion to water is well known, but this doesn't mean they cannot act as a companion on a boat. But training will be required, and being intrinsically less obedient than dogs, cats may need to be corralled well in advance of setting off on the next leg of a cruise if you don't want to hang around waiting for them to come home after a towpath foray. The same logic applies during a cruise – you don't want to draw up at a mooring only to find your cat jumped ship earlier in the day and now could be anywhere within a ten-mile radius. Once again, a tag with essential details is a must. It's also a good idea to check that they haven't chosen the engine compartment as a convenient place for a nap before you set off.

Finally, perhaps the greatest survival tip of all is to recognise that however much you might appreciate your own company, becoming a liveaboard brings with it membership of a wider community. How actively you choose to participate in this community is up to you, but those who ignore it altogether tend to end up being the losers.

Being a liveaboard will mean there will be times when you will need to give and receive favours or just need someone else to talk to, and this will mean tapping into the wider network of like-minded souls. The liveaboard community acts as an informal network which includes those close to you, such as your neighbours, as well as more virtual members, such as other liveaboards you may only see occasionally but keep in touch with. Taken together, this community represents a vast body of knowledge, experience and society you will not want to isolate yourself from, and indeed hopefully will want to contribute to. Successful liveaboards tend to be those who get the personal balance right between enjoying the freedom living on board a boat offers with the benefits of being part of a wider body of people.

Learn More & Links

ORGANISATIONS

There's a wealth of information out there available from the various organisations representing different parts of our waterways, with the following amongst the most significant:

ASSOCIATION OF WATERWAYS CRUISING CLUBS

Focuses on emergency help and overnight moorings for members of affiliated clubs.

26 Cudham Lane North, Cudham, Sevonoaks, Kent TN14 7QS
Tel: 01689 862046 Website: www.awcc.org.uk

BRITISH MARINE FEDERATION

Covers the British marine and leisure industry.

Marine House, Thorpe Lea Road, Egham, Surrey TW20 8BF
Tel: 01784 473377 Website: www.britishmarine.co.uk

BRITISH WATERWAYS

Responsible for the canals.

Willow Grange, Church Road, Watford, Herts WD1 3QA
Tel: 01923 201120 Website: www.britishwaterways.co.uk

THE BROADS AUTHORITY

Responsible for the Broads.

18 Colegate, Norwich, Norfolk NR3 1BQ
Tel: 01603 610734 Website: www.broads-authority.gov.uk

DUTCH BARGE ASSOCIATION

For anyone interested in or who owns a barge.

PO Box 484, Rickmansworth, Herts WD3 1PG
Tel: 07000 227437 Website: www.barges.org

THE ENVIRONMENT AGENCY

Responsible for inland rivers.

National Customer Contact Centre, PO Box 544, Rotherham S60 1BY
Tel: 08708 506506 Website: www.environment-agency.gov.uk

INLAND WATERWAYS ASSOCIATION

Advocate for securing the future of the waterways.

PO Box 114, Rickmansworth, Herts WD3 1ZY
Tel: 01923 711114 Website: www.waterways.org.uk

NATIONAL ASSOCIATION OF BOAT OWNERS

Represents private boat owners.

Freepost (BM8367), Birmingham B31 2BR
Website: www.nabo.org.uk

RESIDENTIAL BOAT OWNERS ASSOCIATION

Represents liveaboard boaters and also publish useful booklets on living aboard
and on council tax.

PO Box 518, Rickmansworth, Herts WD3 1WJ
Website: www.rboa.org.uk

ROYAL YACHTING ASSOCIATION

Represents pleasure boating.

RYA House, Ensign Way, Hamble, Southampton, Hampshire SO31 4YA
Tel: 023 8060 4100 Website: www.rya.org.uk

WATERWAY RECOVERY GROUP

Dedicated to restoring derelict canals.

PO Box 114, Rickmansworth, WD3 1ZY
Tel: 01923 711114 Website: www.wrg.org.uk

THE YACHT HARBOUR ASSOCIATION

Website: www.yachtharbourassociation.com

WEBSITES

The following is a selection of the many waterway-related sites on the web:

www.livingonboats.co.uk – useful site with some good articles on specific issues
www.britishwaterways.co.uk – British Waterways
www.waterscape.com – British Waterways' leisure site which also includes a lot of
practical information on boating in general
www.canalmedia.co.uk – general resources

www.canals.com – comprehensive site on all things to do with canals
www.jim-shead.co.uk – site for one of the UK's most informed canal advocates
www.justcanals.com – claims to list most canal sites
www.leesan.com - for more on toilet options – includes a handy list of pump-out
    locations
www.canaljunction.com/boat/electrics.htm – list of marine electrical and electronic
    equipment suppliers and engineers
www.canaljunction.com/boat/systems.htm#plum – list of suppliers of boat heating,
    water, gas and sanitation suppliers and engineers

BOOKS

The following is a brief selection of waterways-related books. For a more
comprehensive list go to: www.iwashop.com

General

Britain's Canals: A Handbook: Nick Corble (Tempus, 2007)
Canal Boats and Barges: Tony Condor (Shire Books, 2004)
Colours of the Cut: Edward Paget-Tomlinson, A. Lewery (Landscape Press, 2004)
Wildlife of Rivers and Canals: Tony Hopkins and Pat Brassley (Morland Pub. Co., 1982)

Practicalities

The 12 Volt Bible for Boats: Miner Brotherton and Ed Sherman (Thomas Reed
    Publications, 2003)
Boatowner's Wiring Manual: Charles Wing (Adlard Coles Nautical, 1993)
Boat Joinery and Cabinetmaking Simplified: Fred Bingham (McGraw Hill, 2007)
Canal and River Cruising: The IWA Manual: Sheila Davenport (Fernhurst Books, 1998)
The Fibreglass Boat Repair Manual: Allan H. Vaitses (McGraw Hill, 2007)
Fitting Out Your Boat, Fibreglass or Wood: Michael Naujok (Adlard Coles Nautical,
    2004)
Handmade Houseboats: Russell Condor (McGraw Hill, 2007)
A Home Afloat – Stories of Living Aboard Vessels of all Shapes and Sizes: Gary
    Cookson (20/21, 2005)
The Inland Waterways Manual: Emrhys Barrell (Adlard Coles Nautical, 2001)
The Inland Boat Owner's Book: Andrew Burnett (Waterways World, 2000)
Inland Cruising – Practical Course Notes: (Royal Yachting Association, 1995)
The Liveaboard Report – A Boat Dweller's Guide to What Works and What Doesn't:
    Charlie Wing (McGraw Hill, 2007)
Living Afloat: C. Valerie Lee and Beryl McDowall (RBOA, 2007)
The Narrowboat Builder's Book: Graham Booth and Andy Burnett (Waterways
    World, 1999)
Narrow Boats Care and Maintenance: Nick Billingham (Helmsman Books, 1995)
Narrowboat Planning – Designing the Interior of Your Boat: Graham Booth
    (Waterways World, 2005)
The New Narrowboat Builder's Book (Waterways World, 1993)
Simple Boat Electrics: John Myatt (Fernhurst Books, 1997)
Simple Boat Maintenance: Pat Manley (Fernhurst Books, 2005)